SoulStrife

SoulStrife

The *Psychomachia* of Aurelius Prudentius Clemens

Translated with notes
by

William Levitan

FRANCISCAN UNIVERSITY PRESS

Copyright © 2025 by Franciscan University Press
All rights reserved.
No part of this publication may be reproduced or transmitted in any form or means, electronic or mechanical, including photography, recording, or any other information storage or retrieval system, without permission in writing from the publisher. Requests for permission to make copies of any part of the work should be directed to:

Franciscan University Press
1235 University Boulevard
Steubenville, OH 43952
740-283-3771

Distributed by:
The Catholic University of America Press
c/o HFS
P.O. Box 50370
Baltimore, MD 21211
800-537-5487

Cataloging-in-Publication Data available from the Library of Congress

Jacket and Interior Design by Reflective Book Design.
Jacket art: (*front—placard*) From the British Library Collection, Cotton MS Titus D XVI, f. 6r; (*front—background*) From the British Library Collection, Cotton MS Titus D XVI, f. 7r; (*back—background*) From the British Library Collection: Cotton MS Titus D XVI f. 5v.
Printed in the United States of America.

ISBN: 979-8-89372-110-2

For
Martha Malamud

Contents

SoulStrife

CONTENTS

Introduction

Aurelius Prudentius Clemens was born in 348 CE in northern Spain and died sometime after 405 CE. These dates mean that he was an adult when the Edict of Thessalonica established the Trinitarian tenets of the Nicene Creed as the official orthodoxy of the Roman state, when Visigothic armies first began systematic forays into Italy, and during the great inward turn of Christianity. His contemporaries included the prominent contemplatives of the fourth and fifth centuries—the controversial Bishop Athanasius of Alexandria (ca. 298–373); Augustine of Hippo (354–430); Evagrius of Pontus (346–99), author of contemplative manuals for desert monks; and John Cassian (360–435), who brought desert monasticism to the Western Empire—and Prudentius himself was an important interlocutor in the burgeoning discussion about the meaning of Christian life as a form of interiority. His *Psychomachia* in particular offers the reader a guide through an inner struggle, framed primarily as a fight against demons.

Prudentius was active as a classicizing poet at a time when interiority came to the forefront of Christian texts, both written in Greek and translated

The author of this introduction wishes to thank the translator, William Levitan, above all for his engaged, exhilarating translation of this important poem, so restoring its rightful place in Christian literature and late antique Latin poetry for modern readers.

into Latin, as well as composed in Latin: the *Life of Antony* by Athanasius;[1] the *Confessions* of Augustine, the practical and contemplative treatises of Evagrius;[2] and the *Institutes* of Cassian.[3] Prudentius' own exploration of a new Christian interiority was informed at once by classical poetic tropes and by contemporaneous spiritual practices emerging in the fourth century. The unspecified stage on which the battles of the *Psychomachia* take place is precisely the mind's eye, the clear imagination, of every Christian, every reader, and indeed every person; the poem unfolds as development of an interior vision. Since the late fourth century serves as the incipit of what becomes a deeper fathoming of the Christian self, we must look to the inner lives of those who came of age at this time. Prudentius' poem arises in an era that historians[4] have framed in somewhat unflattering terms as the age of a Christian mediocrity, by which they mean that millennialist expectations together with the persecution of Christians disappeared when Christianity became the state religion. But this new status of the Christian religion threw open the question of how the Christian was to live a sanctified and even sacrificial life in relatively safer times.

1. Athanasius published the Greek *Life of Antony* in the fourth century, and it was immediately translated into Latin. A second, more literary translation by Evagrius of Antioch in 373 was rapidly and widely transmitted throughout the Latin West. For the English translation of the Greek text, see William Harmless, "The Life of Antony: Text and Context," in *Desert Christians* (Oxford University Press, 2004.)

2. The Cappadocian transplant Evagrius of Pontus developed an entire system of contemplative prayer which he painstakingly taught for his community in a series of ascetic, moral, and theological tracts, many of these lost. See *Talking Back: A Monastic Handbook for Combating Demons. Evagrius of Pontus*, trans. David Brakke (Cistercian Studies, 2009). See also Robert E. Sinkewicz, *Evagrius of Pontus: The Greek Ascetic Corpus*, Oxford Early Christian Studies (Oxford University Press, 2003). For a scholarly study of the vices in Evagrius, see Leszek Misiarczyk, *Eight Logismoi in the Writings of Evagrius Ponticus* (Brepols, 2021).

3. English translation of Cassian's *Institutes* in C. S. Gibson, *From Nicene and Post-Nicene Fathers*, 2nd ser., vol. 11, ed. Philip Schaff and Henry Wace (Christian Literature Publishing, 1894).

4. E.g., Robert Markus, *The End of Ancient Christianity* (Cambridge University Press, 1990.)

No doubt most influential both on the Christian spiritual renaissance of the fourth century CE and on the actual inner lives of Western Christians is the Greek text, published in Latin translation in 370 CE, of Athanasius of Alexandria's blockbuster narrative, the *Life of Antony* (*Vita Antonii*). The story of Antony's temptations and triumphs in the desert spawned numerous imitations, among which were Jerome's *Life of Paul of Thebes*,[5] whom Jerome billed as the world's first monk. The *Life of Paul* offered an ancient "prequel" (it dates from 375) to the *Vita Antonii*, which Jerome wrote in homage to Athanasius' Antony, the world-renowned Christian action hero who tamed the desert wilderness and established monasteries in the Egyptian desert, while at the same time facing off against the demonic inhabitants who occupied it. Antony's battles against the demons are palpable, audible, and visible; Antony bears the marks of his combat on his flesh, and the sounds of the demons fill his desert redoubt with the snarls of beasts and reptiles (*Vita Antonii* 9). Yet the message of the *Life* is not that the demons rule the desert, but rather that Christ is victorious over the demons, and that Christians participate in that same triumph. The quasi-physical, slapstick, punch-and-drag-out, overwrought quality of these battles, replete with howling demons and all-night vigils, sets the tone for what becomes a formulaic style of hybrid combat against the forces of darkness, inhabiting at once a physical place and yet also entirely lodged within the human soul.

One proof of the power that the *Life of Antony* exercised over Western Christian sensibility is the way that Augustine pays homage to the earlier text in his own spiritual autobiography, *Confessions*. Augustine published

5. For the *Life of Antony*, see Harmless, "Life of Antony." For Jerome's *Life of Paul of Thebes*, see Caroline White's translation in *Early Christian Lives* (Penguin, 1998).

this narrative circa 398, when he became Bishop of Hippo in North Africa, partly as a way to share his spiritual bona fides with his flock. Yet the *Confessions* themselves constitute a brilliantly original hybrid work, inspired by the Psalms and marked in cadences of prayer that sound like late antique Latin "spoken word," but also infused with mystical texts such as Plotinus' (d. 270 CE) own record of spiritual experiences. Having secured a sinecure as a professor of rhetoric in Milan, where Augustine arrived at the age of 30 with mistress and son in tow, Augustine was entering into what looked like a trajectory of worldly success, playing the part of liberal intellectual: Manichee, Platonist, and Christian-curious. Decisive in Augustine's sudden conversion, which involved the dismissal of his life partner, his own baptism, and the abrupt abandonment of his secure post, was Augustine's encounter with the *Life of Antony*. Augustine is brought to his knees over his own vacillations after hearing the story of the putatively illiterate Egyptian Antony's home-leaving, and he is visited with a child's voice who commands, *tolle, lege* (take up and read) (*Conf.* 8.12). He is drawn to open the Bible, and the passage he reads from St. Paul's *Letter to the Romans* dissolves his hesitations.[6] The *Confessions*, a prose poem addressed to God but laying open Augustine's struggle with his own conflicting beliefs, his attachment to pleasure, and his intellectual pride, anticipates Prudentius' *Psychomachia* in its dramatization of the soul's inward evolution toward a Christian identity.

Thus by the time Prudentius wrote the *Psychomachia*, Egyptian monasticism began to seep into Western consciousness via texts such as the Athanasius' *Vita Antonii*, Jerome's *Life of Paul of Thebes*, and Palladius' *Lausiac*

6. *Confessions* 8.14 tells how Pontitianus visited Augustine and shared the story of Antony, "the Egyptian monk, whose name was in high repute among Your servants, though up to that time not familiar to us."

History, written in 419–20. The *Lausiac History* (consisting in stories of the desert hermits) was translated twice into Latin and found great popularity among lay Christians. Note that Antony shows up in all of this later literature, again a testimony to the powerful influence of the *Life*, which Augustine would have read in a Latin translation of Athanasius' Greek original. A monasticism, profoundly inspired by these models, was inchoate in the Western Empire, while the seeds of asceticism had been planted a century earlier, first in the Egyptian desert and then in Palestine, only to flower and fruit in the West through the direct inoculation of Augustine as well as the Egyptian pilgrim, John Cassian, founder of the Abbey of St. Victor in 415 and student of Evagrius, the great desert mystic. Monasticism as a way of life, as a full-time pursuit of inner pathways, came into its own amidst new discourses of self-illumination, including, I would argue, the *Psychomachia*.

In short, the poem *Psychomachia* converged with the growing practice of spiritual struggle as the new Christian "day to day." But just what could be the end or goal of this struggle? A new paradigm for Christian virtue, *hesychia*, inner stillness, the power of peace within,[7] developed from a confluence of traditions, including the Stoic virtue of *apatheia* (passionlessness) and the increasing fame of desert saints. This powerful blend of Stoic detachment, which had earlier steeped into the popular philosophy of the empire (via Epictetus and Seneca), together with the lore surrounding great battles fought in the desert, made possible the imitation of the monk's efforts to still the mind and empty the heart of its own productions in the collective

7. Hesychasm, the name that is still attached to a living tradition of prayer in Eastern Orthodox Christianity and was in antiquity especially prominent in monasteries of Egypt, Palestine, and Greece, consisted in faith in a communal life that centered around the cultivation of inner peace through the solitary recitation of the Jesus prayer and other ascetic practices.

Christian imaginary. It was in Roman Egypt that this tradition took shape, in the deserts near Alexandria, up from the Nile Delta, in monasteries and anchorite retreats, teaching the larger Roman world the meaning of asceticism. *Ascesis*, the athletic discipline of the entire self, trained the contestants for holiness in the taming of both body and mind, helping them to shed the conventional trappings of social norms, and ultimately to separate themselves from their worldly selves, the "old" or "outer" person. Most important in the monk's arsenal were fasting, the weakening of the body and its desires, together with prayer, which reshaped the mind of the practitioner, not so much to embrace an ideology as to rid itself of its moorings in the *mos maiorum*. In the desert, monks practiced the Jesus prayer: *kurie, eleison* (Lord, have mercy) or in its more elaborate form, "Lord Jesus Christ, have mercy upon me, a sinner." The labor of prayer, the single-minded devotion of the monk to the repetition of Jesus' name, banished the habitual thoughts that ensconced the heart in self-interest, in pride and ambition. The Egyptian desert, far from being a wilderness, instead became a city of holy people dwelling in the caves of Nitria, the White Monastery of Shenoute, the Kellia of Evagrius. These two weapons, fasting and prayer, could slay, quite literally, the demons of vice who assailed the monastic by day and night, those duplicitous enemies of salvation who managed to insinuate themselves into the very self through the crevices of thoughts, desires, and the senses. Demon slaying, which wrestled with the aspects of self that were at root alien because they divided the heart, scattered its focus, and obscured the self-luminous grace of divine presence, became the great warfare of the desert, the inner martial art of the master of prayer and his (or her, for there were Desert Mothers) vehicle for liberation. Readers of the *Psychomachia*, a poem credited with the invention of an abstract interior space, will note that Prudentius begins his poem with an exhortation to battle against demons. Levitan's translation reads:

> ABRAM summoned us to war
> Against ungodly tribes,
> For no child of wedlock,
> Conceived in Virtue
> And pleasing to God,
> Is begotten or born
> Until the battling spirit
> With grim and mighty slaughter
> Has conquered the monsters
> Of the heart enslaved.

Who are these monsters that show up in the text? And what ambient factors, poetic and otherwise, went in to their depiction? Readers will notice borrowings from some of Virgil's splendid creations, Fama, Allecto, and even Dido; they will also notice caricatures of Vice leaning on the diatribes of Juvenal and other satirists.[8] Beyond this literary frame, it would seem that the *Psychomachia*, perhaps miraculously, translated the practice of spiritual warfare, the battle between the divine and that which opposes it, into the story of Everyman's inner life. The founder of the order of St. Benedict and the person who single-handedly translated the monastic practices of Egypt into

8. The poem, it has been frequently noted, is funded to some extent by battle scenes of Virgil's *Aeneid*. For detailed comparisons and close readings of *Psychomachia* and the *Aeneid* see Martha A. Malamud, A *Poetics of Transformation* (Cornell University Press, 1989), chap. 3, "Words at War."

a rule for Western monastics was John Cassian. Of Cassian David Brakke writes: "Cassian subordinates the monk's conflict with demons to a persistent and divinely planned conflict within himself."[9] The spiritual warfare that Prudentius reveals in his poem of the same name arose in the ambience of fourth century's fixation on warring virtues and vices, described by the Cappadocian desert transplant, Evagrius, illustrated in the narrative of Augustine's *Confessions* of the boy miscreant who threw away his innocence, and heard in the howls of demons who attacked Antony in his seclusion.

Investigating the action of the poem—the spiritual combat, the strife in and of the soul—we find that it falls into two halves: six combats proceed as a sequence of duels, led by True Faith, at the vanguard of the troops who muster under the banner of virtue, facing off against Idolatry, or Worship of the Ancient Gods, as Prudentius calls her. A train of champions for the side of vice storm the soul in fierce succession: Lust yields to Chastity, Anger falls to Patience, Pride is dispatched by Humility, Luxury is slain by Sobriety, Greed succumbs to Benevolence. In the Latin of Prudentius we have *Fides, Pudicitia, Patientia, Mens Humilis, Sobrietas, Operatio,* and *Concordia* against the seven Vices, *Veterum Cultura Deorum, Libido, Ira, Superbia, Luxuria, Avaritia,* and *Discordia*. Punctuating these combats are harangues set with exemplary biblical characters who provide the template of action evinced by the Virtues themselves: Judith, Job, Adam, Judah, Jonathan, and David. After the virtues achieve victory in the ring, a new, greater danger, that of Discord, imperils the soul's hard won Peace. When the soul has finally set aside Division and Conflict, Peace and Concord build the new Jerusalem, a temple of Wisdom, replete with the precious stones of *Revelation*, within the soul. The struggles

9. David Brakke, *Demons and the Making of the Monk* (Harvard University Press, 2006).

between Virtue and Vice, the victory of Peace, and the temple of Wisdom all follow the pattern of the contemplative path set forth by the Hesychasts and formalized in the work of Evagrius, as we shall see. The celebration of peace toward the end of the poem, in Levitan's translation,

> The fullness of a Virtue's work is PEACE.
> PEACE is the perfection of our labors,
> The prize of the war we waged
> And the dangers we faced.
> In PEACE stars live and move across the sky …
> The proper worship of God begins with PEACE;
> No sacrifice is sweeter to CHRIST,
> No offering more acceptable at his altar.

speaks clearly to the practice of *hesychia* in the terms of a labor, the war "of … light and shadow … within us," that sets the foundation for the flowering of wisdom in the soul, with which the poem ends: "Rich WISDOM! May she reign forever on her splendid throne."

The steps on the path to a purer inner life—namely, using the demonic powers against themselves; countering the forces of greed, anger, and pride with generosity, patience, and humility; unifying the soul; and then allowing wisdom to dawn—are well traveled by the contemplatives, those who cultivate stillness, who devote themselves to peace. The stages traversed within the path outlined by the *Psychomachia* correspond to a recognizable discipline of prayer; they encompass the inner life of a new direction in consciousness, one that both wafted over from the desert and was simultaneously universal: to fully transform the demonic through precise attention to its presence within the heart.

Evagrius Ponticus, to take the example of master of the Hesychast movement who directly influenced Cassian and left copious instructions for those who would set themselves upon this path, set forth a system for such combatants, which he divided into the practical life and the contemplative life proper, both crucial elements for the life of prayer, corresponding to the six battles and the erection of the temple to wisdom in Prudentius' poem. The practical life involves working with the eight thoughts (in Greek, *logismoi*), as Evagrius called them, although he also called them demons: gluttony, impurity, avarice, sadness, anger, *acedia* (sloth), vanity, and pride.[10] They do not exactly correspond to the vices mentioned by Prudentius, but in large measure they do comprise aspects of the self that must be recognized and met with the force of virtues such as patience, love, sobriety, zeal, and humility.[11] The goal of the practical life is, for Evagrius, tranquility, peace, or what he calls *apatheia*, no longer being subject to the demons of vice. But the goal of the contemplative life, once tranquility has taken root, is wisdom. The practitioner must rely on the words of Scripture, as it were, to talk back to the evil suggestions of the demons, those thoughts whose presence tricks the practitioner into thinking that they truly belong to him. Hence Evagrius wrote a manual titled *Antirhetikos*,[12] or "Talking Back," a guide to using quotations from Scripture to overpower the force of the demons, rather than relying on one's own inventions.

10. Robert E. Sinkewicz, *Evagrius of Pontus: The Greek Ascetic Corpus*, Oxford Early Christian Studies (Oxford University Press, 2003).

11. On Evagrius' "eight thoughts" and the seven deadly sins, see Richard Sorabji, *Emotion and Peace of Mind: From Stoic Agitation to Christian Temptation* (Oxford University Press, 2000), 358–59.

12. Evagrius, *A Monastic Handbook for Combating Demons*, trans. David Brakke, Cistercian Studies Series 229 (Liturgical Press, 2009).

Although in Prudentius the contrast between figural representation of biblical characters and genuine personification can be discerned when Prudentius reverts to biblical scenes, it must be understood that the divine *logos*, which for Prudentius augmented and suffused human nature, is always the greatest champion and final protector of the human soul.

Prudentius' systematic study of how to counter demonic states with the energy that can oppose them, the virtues, owes something to Stoicism and its negative characterization of the passions as rooted in false thoughts and as the enemy of wisdom. Certainly, Stoicism developed one of the most elaborate and effective series of what Hadot called "Spiritual Exercises," or meditations, contemplative practices, among all the ancient schools.[13] Working with the passions precisely through an understanding of their underlying nature as false thought constructions that obscure the clarity of reason was one of the chief burdens of such systems as one finds in Marcus Aurelius' *Meditations* or Cicero's earlier *Tusculan Disputations*. Early Christian psychology, particularly as we discover it in Origen's (d. 253 CE) discussion of sin, is dependent on the Stoic conception of the development of passion from what he calls *logismoi* (thoughts; in Rufinus' Latin translation, *cogitationes*). Origen writes: "we find that the thoughts (*cogitationes*) which proceed from our heart, whether they are a memory of some actions or a contemplation of things and their causes, sometimes come from us ourselves, sometimes are stirred up by hostile powers, and sometimes are introduced even by God or the holy angels."[14]

And the Origenist treatment of thoughts that arise from the heart,

13. See Pierre Hadot, *Philosophy as a Way of Life: Spiritual Exercises from Socrates to Foucault*, trans. Michael Chase (Blackwell, 1995).

14. Origen, *On First Principles*, 3.2.4. Quoted and translated by Sorabji, *Emotion and Peace of Mind*, 347.

possibly under the influence of maleficent forces, directly influenced Evagrius' doctrine of the seven deadly sins. In calling all of these iterations of the inner battle (the psychomachia proper and not just the poem) systematic, I mean both that the Stoics organized the treatment of passions according to genus and species, and that the techniques for diminishing their strength, such as calling upon the power of God's name, or opposing a virtue to a given vice, or stilling the mind so that one can see more clearly, were systematically laid out in the handbooks of late antiquity, from Seneca's *Letters to Lucilius*, to Epictetus' *Enchiridion*, to Evagrius' *Praktikos*.[15]

In addition to the abstract philosophical ideas that the poem touches on, the real engine of the work is its devotional or contemplative deployment in the imagination of the reader who can use the words of Prudentius to pay attention to what is going on in her own soul, to gain insight, through self-awareness, into her own traffic in those universal distractions, which in the tradition of Christian contemplative psychology are no longer so innocent. Rather, ordinary thoughts of lust, anger, hate, and boredom are symptoms of the demonic. Prudentius literally suggests that what passes for ordinary human life is in actuality the work of monsters.

Let us briefly reference another of Prudentius' poems, the *Hamartigenia* (*Origin of Sin*), a poem in hexameters designed to confute heretics. This poem actually astonishes the reader with a graphic genealogy of what he calls "a brood of vipers," "a deadly race," referring to the origins of vice in the soul. The *Psychomachia* teaches the soul to fight back against the monstrous infestation. The *Hamartigenia* reads like a science fiction film script, as the alien larvae of vice nest and then consume the womb of the innocent soul:

15. Sorabji, *Emotion and Peace of Mind*, 303–18.

> At last, as their nurturing mother dies, the brood
> of sorrows emerges, barely forcing their way
> out into life, carving out their birth
> by crime. The puppies creep about and lick
> the corpse that bore them—a generation orphaned
> at birth, bereft of their poor mother before
> they ever saw the light of day. The way
> our soul conceives is not dissimilar: in just
> this way, with Belial as mate, the soul
> guzzles venom gushing from the viper's
> mouth and sucks his kisses down and draws
> them deep inside.[16]

We can imagine Prudentius' readers disturbed, to say the least, by the *Hamartigenia*'s frightening image of a festering clutch of parasites, ready to consume the soul.[17] The *Psychomachia*, then, is strong medicine against internal parasites, functioning somewhat like the white blood cells of virtue, rushing to protect the infected blood of the Christian collective body:

> Speak to us, King, and tell us what soldiery
> The mind can muster in its war with Sin;

16. Prudentius, *The Origin of Sin*, trans. Martha A. Malamud (Cornell University Press, 2011), 793*ff*.

17. On the *Psychomachia* as a kind of practical manual for the doctrine of sin to be found in the *Hamartigenia*, see Michele Cutino, "Les phases du combat spirituel dans la Psychomachia de Prudence," *Revue des études anciennes* 112, no. 1 (2010): 37–53; Kathleen Kirsch, "Reconsidering the Monsters of Prudentius's Psychomachia," *Journal of Late Antiquity* 13, no. 2 (2020): 220–33.

When thoughts turn rebel and passionate Strife
Assails the Soul, tell us what defense there is
That will secure her liberty; and tell us,
Good Commander, what force will overwhelm
The maniac Commotions of the heart.
For you have not exposed the Christian people
To the ravages of Sin without resource,
Without the strength derived from the great Virtues.

At the beginning of his poem, Prudentius tells the reader, "And the way of our victory is clear Once we see clear the true faces of the Virtues And the monsters that are their deadly enemies." Thus the poem is in and of itself a tool for attention; it allows us to see what is within ourselves. And that vision, in turn, becomes the jewel of wisdom with which the poem ends. The pragmatic, illative force of this poem, whose power is conveyed through the sheer violence of battle, calls forth a surge of attention, and that attention is then harnessed as a field of awareness in which the practitioner now lives. In time, through attention, the energy of the psyche shifts and aligns itself with the virtues, led by faith followed by patience, which together slow the pull of the demonic desires and destructive anger that perpetuates the false self, the one that thinks it is nothing but the den of demons and forgets its true nature, self-luminous, divinely wrought, a jewel of wisdom in the crown of glory that the true sons (and daughters) of the church are called to wear.

The poem's clarity and lucidity, once obscured to the English reader by lesser translations, are now laid bare through the precise and artful translation of William Levitan. Because of this translation, the reader's encounter with the *Psychomachia* still has the force intended by its author. The poem is anything but cliché, stagnant, or an aesthetic failure. It is a vehicle that attempts to convey the contemplative path and that calls the soul home, to its genuine place of rest, to the stillness of prayer and the abiding grace of Wisdom.

Sara Ahbel-Rappe

UNIVERSITY OF MICHIGAN

True Faith addresses the Virtues. *Lyon, Bibliothèque de la Part-Dieu, P. A. 22, f. 12v (photo: IRHT-CNRS)*

Suggestions for Further Reading

Auerbach, Erich. 1944. "Figura." In *Neue Dantestudien*, 11–71. Basimevi. Trans. Ralph Manheim in Auerbach, 1959, *Scenes from the Drama of European Literature*, 11–76. Meridian.

Auerbach, Erich. 1993. *Literary Language and Its Public in Late Latin Antiquity and in the Middle Ages*. Princeton University Press.

Berno, Francesca Romana. 2023. *Roman Luxuria: A Literary and Cultural History*. Oxford University Press.

Blackburn, Simon. 2004. *Lust: The Seven Deadly Sins*. Oxford University Press.

Bloomfield, Morton. 1952. *The Seven Deadly Sins*. Michigan State College Press.

Brown, Peter. 1971. *The World of Late Antiquity: AD 150–750*. Thames and Hudson.

Brown, Peter. 2008. *The Body and Society: Men, Women, and Sexual Renunciation in Early Christianity*. 2nd ed. Columbia University Press.

Burroughs, William S. 1991. *The Seven Deadly Sins*. Lococo-Mulder.

Cameron, Alan. 1970. *Claudian: Poetry and Propaganda at the Court of Honorius*. Oxford University Press.

Cameron, Alan. 2011. *The Last Pagans of Rome*. Oxford University Press.

Carruthers, Mary. 1990. *The Book of Memory: A Study of Memory in Medieval Culture*. Cambridge University Press.

SUGGESTIONS FOR FURTHER READING

Carruthers, Mary. 1998. *The Craft of Thought: Meditation, Rhetoric, and the Making of Images, 400–1200*. Cambridge University Press.

Conybeare, Catherine. 2013. *The Laughter of Sarah: Biblical Exegesis, Feminist Theory, and the Concept of Delight*. Palgrave Macmillan.

Copeland, Rita, and Peter Struck, eds. 2010. *The Cambridge Companion to Allegory*. Cambridge University Press.

Curtius, E. R. 1953. *European Literature and the Latin Middle Ages*. Trans. W. R. Trask. Princeton University Press.

Dawson, David. 2002. *Christian Figural Reading and the Fashioning of Identity*. University of California Press.

Dodds, E. R. 1965. *Pagan and Christian in an Age of Anxiety*. Cambridge University Press.

Dyson, Michael Eric. 2006. *Pride: The Seven Deadly Sins*. Oxford University Press.

Gassman, Mattias P. 2020. *Worshippers of the Gods: Debating Paganism in the Fourth Century Roman West*. Oxford University Press.

Hershkowitz, Paula. 2017. *Prudentius, Spain, and Late Antique Christianity: Poetry, Visual Culture, and the Cult of the Martyrs*. Cambridge University Press.

Katzenellenbogen, Adolf. 1964. *Allegories of the Virtues and Vices in Medieval Art*. W. W. Norton.

Kirsch, Kathleen. 2020. "Reconsidering the Monsters of Prudentius' *Psychomachia*." *Journal of Late Antiquity* 13, no. 3: 220–33.

Leatherbury, Sean Villareal. 2020. *Inscribing Faith in Late Antiquity: Between Reading and Seeing*. Routledge.

Lewis, C. S. 1936. *The Allegory of Love: A Study in Medieval Tradition*. Clarendon Press.

Lowe, D. M. 2008. "Personification Allegory in the *Aeneid* and Ovid's *Metamorphoses*." *Mnemosyne* 61, no. 3: 414–35.

Malamud, Martha A. 1989. *A Poetics of Transformation: Prudentius and Classical Mythology*. Cornell University Press.

Malamud, Martha A. 2011. *The Origin of Sin: An English Translation of the* Hamartigenia. Cornell University Press.

Mastrangelo, Marc. 2008. *The Roman Self in Late Antiquity: Prudentius and the Poetics of the Soul.* Johns Hopkins University Press.

Mastrangelo, Marc. 2022. *Prudentius'* Psychomachia. Routledge.

Miller, Patricia Cox. 2001. *The Poetry of Thought in Late Antiquity: Essays in Imagination and Religion.* Ashgate.

Miller, Patricia Cox. 2009. *The Corporeal Imagination: Signifying the Holy in Late Ancient Christianity.* University of Pennsylvania Press.

Nugent, S. Georgia. 1985. *Allegory and Poetics: The Structure and Imagery of Prudentius'* Psychomachia. Peter Lang.

Paxson, J. J. 1994. *The Poetics of Personification.* Cambridge University Press.

Pelttari, Aaron. 2019. *The* Psychomachia *of Prudentius: Text, Commentary, and Glossary*. University of Oklahoma Press.

Roberts, Michael. 1989. *The Jeweled Style: Poetry and Poetics in Late Antiquity.* Cornell University Press.

Sayers, Dorothy L. 1943. *The Other Six Deadly Sins: An Address Given to the Public Morality Council at Caxton Hall, Westminster, on October 23rd, 1941.* Methuen.

Shanzer, D. 1989. "Allegory and Reality: Spes, Victoria, and the Date of Prudentius' *Psychomachia.*" *Illinois Classical Studies* 14: 347–63.

Smith, Macklin. 1976. *Prudentius'* Psychomachia: *A Reexamination.* Princeton University Press.

Struck, Peter. 2004. *Birth of the Symbol: Readers at the Limits of Their Texts.* Princeton University Press.

Thomson, H. J., ed. and trans. 1949–53. *Prudentius.* 2 vols. Harvard University Press.

Tickle, Phyllis A. 2004. *Greed: The Seven Deadly Sins.* Oxford University Press.

Woodruff, Helen. 1930. *The Illustrated Manuscripts of Prudentius.* Harvard University Press.

SoulStrife

FOREWORD

Abraham. *Lyon, Bibliothèque de la Part-Dieu, P. A. 22, f. 2r (photo: IRHT-CNRS)*

Foreword

Abram

The name Abram in Hebrew means Exalted Father, and the name Abraham, Father of Multitudes.

Patriarch of faith,
Pioneer in belief,
Father late in life
Of blessed generations;
Called Abram by his father,
Renamed Abraham by God,
His name augmented
By a syllable;
Who offered his son
To God in sacrifice,
Showing that sacrifice
Must offer freely
What is sweet, what is loved,
What cannot be replaced—

Abram summoned us to war
Against ungodly tribes,
For no child of wedlock,

A conjunction of Abraham's literal paternity at age 100 (Genesis 21:5) and the symbolic paternity ascribed to him by Paul: "They who are of faith . . . are the children of Abraham"(Galatians 3:7).

Genesis 17:5

Genesis 22

The captivity of Lot. *London, from the British Library Collection, Cotton MS Cleopatra C VIII, f. 4v*

Conceived in Virtue
And pleasing to God,
Is begotten or born
Until the battling spirit
With grim and mighty slaughter
Has conquered the monsters
Of the heart enslaved.

This he argued by his own example.

THE CAPTIVITY AND LIBERATION OF LOT

Genesis 14

For it happened that his nephew,
LOT, had fallen into the hands
Of savage kings, invaders
Of Sodom and Gomorrah,
Where he had been dwelling,
A sojourner among them;
And LOT was led away in chains,
A slave to foreign lords.

Then ABRAM armed
Three hundred eighteen
Slaves born to his house
And ordered them to fall upon

Working out of both Jewish and Hellenistic traditions of textual exegesis, Philo of Alexandria (ca. 20 BCE to 40 CE) also read the episode of Lot's captivity as an allegory of moral struggle. Philo took the five cities of the plain of Sodom to represent the five senses; the invading kings the four passions of grief, fear, pleasure, and desire; and Abraham the intervention of corrective reason, which "when it has taken up the full weaponry of the virtues ... conquers all things.... [T]he nine kingdoms of the four passions and five senses are perishable.... But as the tenth, a perfect number, the divine word ...

(continued on p. 6)

The enemy on the march,
Now slow and encumbered
With the spoils of war.
Then, filled with his God,
He unsheathed his sword
And put those kings to rout
And slaughtered them as they fled
And trampled them as they lay
Broken beneath his feet.
Now he shatters the bonds,
Releases the captive treasure—
Cattle and horses,
Girls and young children,
Gold, jewels, rich silks—
And LOT in his freedom
Straightens his neck
Where chains have rubbed it raw.

So ABRAM returned in glory,
His brother's son restored:
No violence of vicious kings
Could check
A child of faithful stock.

(continued from p. 5)
subdues all the other powers by its force when it descends into the conflict and exerts the greater power which it has in accordance with God" (De Abrahamo 243–44).

In a similar but simpler vein, Ambrose, Bishop of Milan (d. 397), allegorized Abraham as Mind (Latin MENS*) that conduces to virtue and linked his paternal status to this function, "in that the entire person is governed by the authority, judgment, and care of a fatherly mind"* (De Abraham 2.1.1).

Abram in arms. *London, from the British Library Collection, Cotton MS Cleopatra C VIII, f. 5r*

Sarah laughs in disbelief. *Lyon, Bibliothèque de la Part-Dieu, P. A. 22, f. 5r* (*photo: IRHT-CNRS*)

THE PRIEST MELCHIZEDEK

The name Melchizedek in Hebrew means Righteous King.

And as he came in triumph,
Still bloodstained from the slaughter,
A priest gave him sustenance
Of heaven, a priest of God
But a king, too, in that land,
MELCHIZEDEK, whose line
Remains unknown
Except to the one God.
Then a trinity of angels
Came to ABRAM, guests
In the old man's ger.

Genesis 14:17–19, Hebrews 7:1–2

Some manuscripts include these verses:

"Whose birth is unrevealed,
Whose source cannot be named."

The unobtrusive silence of Genesis about the priest's family is understood by Hebrews 7:3 as an indication of his mystic origin.

Genesis 18:1–2

SARAH, MOTHER OF ISAAC

And when SARAH quickened,
The gift of youth restored
To her bloodless womb,
And knew she had conceived,
She was amazed,
And she rued her laughter
As she rejoiced in an heir.

Sarah had laughed in disbelief on first hearing of her pregnancy (Genesis 18:10–15), then laughed in joy when her son was born (Genesis 21:7). The name Isaac in Hebrew means Laugh.

Now this line
Was prescribed long ago
For us to follow,

"Now all these things happened to them in figure: and they are written for our correction, upon whom the ends of the world are come."

1 Corinthians 10:11

THE ALLEGORIES OF THE PRESENT FOREWORD

A figure to retrace
With unwavering foot:
Vigilance always
In the armor of faith
Against desires
That enslave us,
Mustering our armies
At home to set us free.
There are forces at the ready
In slaves born to the house
And in the mystic figure
Three hundred eighteen.
Then CHRIST himself,
Who is the True Priest,
Born of the Father,
One and unnamable,
Will offer sustenance
To those who come in triumph,
And he will bless them;
And he will enter the hut
Of the pure and humble heart,
Granting it the honor

"[T]he notion of the new manifestation, the changing aspect, of the permanent runs through the whole history of the word [FIGURA]."

Erich Auerbach, "Figura."

In Greek alphabetic notation, 318 is written TIH, *which was taken to represent the crucified Christ,* T *visually indicating the cross and* IH *being the first letters of the Greek name of Jesus. "It was indicated, accordingly, that Abraham's household slaves were in a state of salvation, … having fled to the Sign and the Name of the Savior" (Clement of Alexandria,* Stromata *6.11).*

An intersection of several texts: Genesis 14:18 with its first, brief mention of Melchizedek; Psalms 110:4, which speaks cryptically about priests "after the order of Melchizedek"; and Hebrews 5:10, 6:20, and 7, which present Melchizedek as a prefiguration of Christ.

Of the Trinity as guest.
Then the Spirit will take
The Soul in his embrace,
The Soul who has been childless
For so long;
And he will make her fruitful
With deathless seed,
And she will become
A mother late in life,
Bringing a worthy heir
To fill the Father's house.

Sarah, read here as the feminine Soul (Latin ANIMA*) impregnated by the masculine Spirit (*SPIRITUS*), had been allegorized by Paul at Galatians 4:21–5:1 as the covenant of the heavenly Jerusalem and "our mother." Paul quoted Isaiah 54:1: "Rejoice, O barren woman, who do not give birth, . . . for many are the children of the woman bereft, more than of her that hath a husband." In his own allegorization, Ambrose identified Sarah as "true virtue, true wisdom"* (De Abraham 2.10.73).

INVOCATION

Christ *Lyon, Bibliothèque de la Part-Dieu, P. A. 22, f. 1v (photo: IRHT-CNRS)*

Invocation

CHRIST, EVER COMPASSIONATE
Toward the grievous suffering of men,
Glorious in your Father's power, and glorious
In your own, though it is a single power,
For we worship a single God under either name,
Single, yet not also solitary
Since from the Father you are God, O CHRIST—

"Phoebus, ever compassionate toward the grievous suffering of Troy. . . ."
Virgil, Aeneid 6.56

CHRIST INVOKED AS THE MUSE OF THE POEM

Speak to us, King, and tell us what soldiery
The mind can muster in its war with Sin;
When thoughts turn rebel and passionate Strife
Assails the Soul, tell us what defense there is
That will secure her liberty; and tell us,
Good Commander, what force will overwhelm
The maniac Commotions of the heart.
For you have not exposed the Christian people
To the ravages of Sin without resource,

"Put on the armor of God, that you may be able to stand against the intrigues of the devil. For we wrestle not against flesh and blood, but against principalities and powers, against the rulers of the world of this darkness, against the spirits of wickedness in high places."
Ephesians 6:11–12

"Let us too conquer all things, not for the prize of a crown or a garland . . . but for virtue, strength of spirit, and a peace that . . . is won forever."
Seneca, Epistulae Morales *78.16*

Without the strength derived from the great Virtues.
No, you yourself lead squadrons to relieve
The flesh besieged, and you yourself have armed
Our inborn nature with abilities
To battle the depravity within,
To struggle for you, to conquer for you.
And the way of our victory is clear
Once we see clear the true faces of the Virtues
And the monsters that are their deadly enemies.

FIRST COMBAT

"If you want combat and struggle, here they are.... Behold Shamelessness thrown down by Chastity, Treachery slain by Faith, Cruelty crushed by Pity, and Impudence cast by Modesty into the shade...."

TERTULLIAN, *DE SPECTACULIS* 29

"I have used similitudes."

HOSEA 12:10, EPIGRAPH OF JOHN BUNYAN, *THE PILGRIM'S PROGRESS*

True Faith and Idolatry. *London, from the British Library Collection, Cotton MS Titus D XVI, f. 5v*

First Combat

TRUE FAITH

TRUE FAITH IS FIRST,
striding forth
Onto the chancy field of war.
Arms and shoulders bare, hair long, uncoiffed,
Stormy in her rugged style,
She wears no armor, carries no weapon,
A ferocious heat
For new battles, new victories,
Her only armament in the coming fight.

IDOLATRY

Now *see*—WORSHIP OF THE ANCIENT GODS
Accepts the challenge; measuring force with force,
She dares the first blow. But TRUE FAITH
Raises herself to her full height
And comes down hard on her enemy's head,
Smashing her to the ground.
The mouth that once was glutted
With the blood of sacrificial animals

"The hero raised himself to his full height and hurled the stone at his enemy."
Virgil, Aeneid *12.901–2, of Turnus in battle with Aeneas*

Is stopped with dirt and stones;
The headbands of her ancient priesthood
Sprawl filthy on the ground.
                                        And now TRUE FAITH
Sets to work in earnest, grinds her heels
In the other's face, squeezing her eyeballs
Out with a dead pop.
                                    Then she crushes the trachea,
And what is left of the fetid breath
Whistles and heaves in the splintered tube:
No leap to death, but a long, agonizing crawl.

"The gods are dead, killed by the one God...."
Ferdinand Lot, The End of the Ancient World

And the army shouts its jubilation;
A thousand martyrs chant the victory
As TRUE FAITH walks among them,
Acknowledging each one.
And she crowns their heads with flowers
According to their merit,
And wraps them all in robes of glowing purple.

Idolatry strikes the first blow. *London, from the British Library Collection, Cotton MS Titus D XVI, f. 5v*

True Faith defeats Idolatry. *London, from the British Library Collection, Cotton MS Titus D XVI, f. 6r*

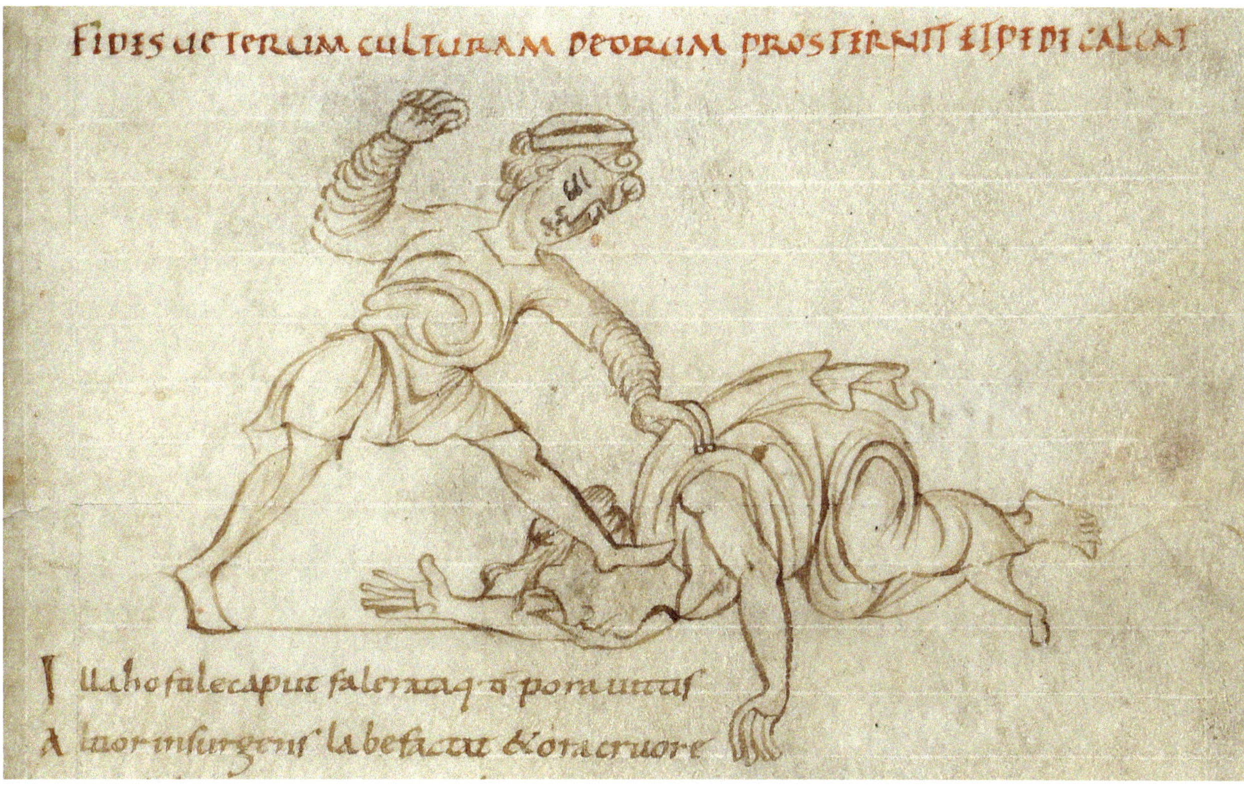

True Faith grinds her heel in Idolatry's face. *Brussels, KBR Ms. 9987-91, f. 103r*

True Faith crowns the martyrs. *London, from the British Library Collection, Cotton MS Cleopatra C VIII, f. 7v*

SECOND COMBAT

Chastity defends herself against Lust. *London, from the British Library Collection, Cotton MS Titus D XVI, f. 7r*

Second Combat

CHASTITY

A GRASSY PLAIN, A GIRL IN READINESS:
The maiden CHASTITY shining in arms.

LUST

And against her, LUST
From Sodom, clothed in the fume and flame
That is her patrimony. On she comes,
Pine torches blazing with brimstone and pitch
To lunge at the young girl's face.
She goes first for the eyes,
Shamefast and brilliant,
Hoping to blind them in the oily smoke.
The girl, though, is steady and with a rock
Strikes the red whip from the whore's right hand.
Then pressing home the point of her sword,
She rams it through the bitch's throat,
Venting a steaming miasma from the lungs
Thick with clotted blood,
And the stench pollutes the nearby air.

Genesis 19:1–29

"Fury attacks, even as Piety shrinks from the sight, withdrawing her shamefast countenance . . . ; and now Fury hurls her torch."
Statius, Thebaid *9.492–95*

THE SPEECH OF CHASTITY

Then the girl in triumph:
"It is over
At last: no more will your deathfires
Threaten the servants of God,
Whose hearts blaze only with the lamp of CHRIST.

JUDITH AND HOLOFERNES

"Enough that you could rise to life again,
Scourgebitch of humankind,
After iron JUDITH sliced the head
From the neck of HOLOFERNES,
Soaking his rubied bed in blood
And composing his passions with the sword.
She carried a noble trophy from the field
That day, heaven's champion and mine.

"But still under the shadow of the Law,
Perhaps the woman did not have the strength
To complete what she'd begun.
Yet she sets the figure for our own times
When the true power
For even the weakest to effect great things
Has passed into earthly bodies.
For now that a virgin has given birth,
What claim can LUST have left to press?

In the Book of Judith, included in the biblical canons of the Catholic and Orthodox Churches, the Israelite widow used her beauty to gain entry to the tent of an invading Assyrian commander. Rather than accede to his desires, she beheaded him with his own sword and returned to her people, carrying high the severed head in triumph.

Chastity refers to the dispensation of the Hebrew Scriptures, the Mosaic Law, imagined as the "shadow" of the Christian revelation to come. Paul's epistles established the trope in such passages as Hebrews 10:1: "For the law having a shadow of the good things to come, not the very image of the things. . . ." In similar language, Tertullian (ca. 160 to ca. 240) described the movement from the Law to Christ as a shift "from shadow to substance, that is, from figures to the truth" (Adversus Marcionem 5.19)*. The usage became commonplace in Christian writings.*

Chastity stabs Lust. *Brussels, KBR Ms. 10066-77, f. 116v*

The combat of Chastity and Lust. *St. Gallen, Stiftsbibliothek, Cod. Sang. 135, p. 391 (www.e-codices.ch/en/list/csg/0135/391)*

THE INCARNATION

Yes, now that the Virgin has given birth,
Human nature is transformed,
And human flesh made new.
An unwed woman conceived the God CHRIST,
Man from his mother, God from the Father.
And the flesh that conceives him is all godly now,
Sharing the nature of God, its partner in union.
The Word Made Flesh has not ceased to be *John 1:14*
What it was, that is, the Word,
Even throughout its tenancy of the flesh;
Nor is its greatness diminished
By the tenancy,
But it raises humankind to nobler things.
He remains what he ever was, even while
He comes to be what he was not.
But what *we* were, we are no more,
Becoming more, augmented by our birth
Into a better state. He has joined unto me
And remained unto himself.
What is his God has not lessened
By assuming what is ours,
But by adding his to ours,
He has brought us to the highest
Of all his heavenly gifts.

Chastity washes her sword in the Jordan. *London, from the British Library Collection, Cotton MS Titus D XVI, f. 8v*

"And now by his gift you lie beaten,
Whore: so die and make an end.
Go! Find the abyss and roll forever
Sunk in its black fire flood.
Become the way to Death, the door to Hell,
And never more try the people of CHRIST
Or corrupt their bodies or infect their souls,
Which they must preserve for their King."

So CHASTITY to filth.
And the girl is glad,
And in triumph takes the triumphant sword
And dips it in the Jordan's waters,
Rinsing it clean of the gristle and gore
That clung to the shining iron,
Fouling it as if with bloodied dew.
Then, deftly, she purifies the cutting edge
In the river's bath, washing away
All stain with this baptism.
The sword, now cleansed,
She does not restore to its customary sheath,
Where rust could mar its splendor;
But in God's universal temple, by the altar
Of God's fountain, she dedicates the blade
Where it will gleam with everlasting light.

THE ALLEGORY OF BAPTISM

Traditional place of baptism. See Matthew 3, Mark 1:5–9, Luke 3:15–21, and John 1:24–34.

"But the water that I shall give him shall be ... a fountain ... springing up into life everlasting." John 4:14

THIRD COMBAT

Anger confronts Patience. *Lyon, Bibliothèque de la Part-Dieu, P. A. 22, f. 4v (photo: IRHT-CNRS)*

Third Combat

Patience

SEE, JUST THERE—SOLEMN, DISCREET,
PATIENCE standing
Unmoved throughout the mayhem,
Watching bodies cut and broken, guts
Run through with iron stakes;
standing and watching,
Inert, eyes fixed.
And in the distance—there!—

Anger

ANGER swells and roils, ill-stomaching
The placid noncombatant.
She rolls her bile-streaked eyes, she bares her teeth,
Spit flies from her mouth.
Tossing the high crests of her helmet,
She shrieks at PATIENCE from across the field:

"Idler! Neutral! Spectator!
Take *this* for your smug indifference—
Death with a hard metal bite.

"Other vices can be concealed and fostered in secret; anger shows itself openly . . . and the greater it is, the more plainly it boils over. See how certain signs appear in all animals before they attack, and how their entire bodies shed their usual appearance and emphasize their ferocity. Boars foam at the mouth and sharpen

(*continued on p. 38*)

"Not even a mediocre gladiator has ever uttered a single groan, has ever altered his countenance, has ever disgraced himself, either on his feet or in his fall."
Cicero, Disputationes Tusculanae 2.41

"Every injury in word or deed that meets with patience will come to the same end as a weapon hurled against a rock. Blunted, it will fall straight to the ground, its action vain and fruitless, or sometimes it will rebound in a counter-attack, working its fury on the very one who threw it."
Tertullian, De Patientia 8.7.

But not a whimper from you: a single groan
Means your disgrace!"

And with that she lets fly a javelin,
Loosed screaming through the air.
And it does not miss its mark but hits PATIENCE
Square in the stomach.
A thud—and the shaft rebounds, thrown back
By the dense resistance of the armor
PATIENCE has hung from her shoulders,
Iron mail wound with oxhide thongs
And a breastplate of adamant three layers thick.

So the foresighted Virtue remains calm,
Stony amid a thundercloud of missiles,
Impenetrably secure. She stands and waits
For ANGER to succumb to her own violence.

Again and again the savage warbitch
Hurls her weapons, and again and again
They fall useless to the ground,
Vain as wind, light as straw, all broken.
At last she takes her sword by the hilt,
Raises it, flashing, high above her ear,

(continued from p. 37)
their teeth by rubbing them against trees, bulls toss their horns in the air and scatter the sand with their feet, lions growl, the necks of angry snakes swell, mad dogs put on a grim expression. There is no beast so frightening by nature that it does not show greater menace when seized by anger. I know that other passions can hardly be hidden . . . for all strong passions affect the countenance. But the difference between them and anger is that while other passions may be visible, anger is conspicuous."
Seneca, De Ira 1.1.5–7

"Sin is a stuck record, round and round, over and over, always the same, and by being always the same, always deader, the smell of decay always heavier. Nothing ever escapes from the Yellow Lagoon of terminal torpor, from the searing erogenous fumes of hermetic Lust, the green acids
(continued on p. 39)

(*continued from p. 38*)
of Envy, the mineral hunger of discarnate Avarice, the Pride that must always excel, the Anger that must blight and kill when there is nothing left to blight or kill, round and round, slower and slower. . . .”
William S. Burroughs, The Seven Deadly Sins

And with all her strength she quickly swings it
Down on her opponent's head.
It strikes just on the center ridge; the helmet's
Furnace-hardened bronze rings under the blow.
But the sword itself rebounds,
Its edge blunted, its steel shivered in pieces,
While the helmet remains unyielding,
Unflinching, and unhurt.

“But the faithless sword shivered in mid stroke. . . .”
Virgil, Aeneid 12.731–32

ANGER sees the fragmentation of her sword,
Feels the weight of the ivory hilt, now lightened
Of its blade, then flings aside the faithless sign
Of honor turned to shame. Now wild, raving,
She burns for her own destruction.
From the many weapons scattered in the dust
She takes up one for an inverted use:
Fixing the spear butt in the ground,
She falls on the upturned point, driving its flange
Deep into her lung.
PATIENCE stands above her:

THE SELF-IMMOLATION OF ANGER

“. . . rushing onto the point of the sword, eager for vengeance even when it drags the avenger along with it.”
Seneca, De Ira 1.1.1

“We have overcome an arrogant Vice
With ordinary virtue. We have lost no blood,
We have risked no life. The rule of our warfare
Is to rout the soldiery of Evil,

Anger strikes Patience. *Lyon, Bibliothèque de la Part-Dieu, P. A. 22, f. 7r* (*photo: IRHT-CNRS*)

Anger self-slain. *Lyon, Bibliothèque de la Part-Dieu, P. A. 22, f. 7v (photo: IRHT-CNRS)*

Anger falls on her sword. *London, from the British Library Collection, Cotton MS Titus D XVI, f. 11r*

To quell its violence and fury,
By our own forbearance. The enemy of Passion
Is that Passion, Frenzy consumes Frenzy,
ANGER turns her weapons inward, on herself."

Now the troops make way for her,
And with her walks an exceptional man;
JOB
For it is JOB who stayed closest to PATIENCE
Throughout every battle. Still haggard,
Worn out from so much death,
He can just begin to smile now,
Remembering his sores, all healed, *Job 2:7*
And the number of his scars
And the ten thousand toils that are his glory
And the discomfiture of his adversaries.
And heavenly PATIENCE bids him rest
Amid fortunes restored twice over *Job 42:10*
And new-won wealth never more to be lost.

"The most trustworthy virtue is that which long and carefully considers itself, controls itself, and slowly and deliberately brings itself to the front."
Seneca, De Ira *1.11.8*

And she herself braves the strife of armies
As she strides through the battle unharmed.
To every Virtue she alone stands as ally,
Sharing her courage and strength. No Virtue
Enters the struggle without her;
Without PATIENCE, every Virtue is bereft.

Patience and Job amid the strife. *St. Gallen, Stiftsbibliothek, Cod. Sang. 135, p. 395 (www.e-codices.ch/en/csg/0135/395)*

FOURTH COMBAT

Pride. *London, from the British Library Collection, Cotton MS Cleopatra C VIII, f. 14r*

Fourth Combat

Pride

"*Pride is the beginning of all sin.*"
Ecclesiasticus 10:15

PRIDE SITS HIGH ON A LION'S PELT
Draped over the back of a mettled steed.
She prances freely across the field,
Looking down on the ranks of the fighters
With swelling disdain.
On her head
An artifice of curls rises sharply
In a tower set above her brow
Dissembling her natural height.
A linen mantle floats from her shoulders,
Gathered in a knot at her breast;
And from her neck a long loose-flowing fringe
Billows like a banner in the wind
And catches every contrary puff of air.

Her horse too is in constant motion
With no less self-regard than PRIDE herself.
It makes a show of resisting constraint—

"*Pride is the commander of the army of the devil, and its offspring are the principal vices. All the vices that assail us are invisible soldiers … in a battle where pride rules over them all; some of these are leaders, others follow as the army. For not all vices take possession of the heart with equal effect. Rather, after a few great faults enter a neglected soul, countless lesser vices pour into it in waves. And pride itself is the queen of the vices; once it has seized and defeated the soul, it turns the battle over to the seven principal vices, as to its officers. Behind these … follow a multitude of other vices which assuredly arise from them.… Truly pride is the root of all evil.…*"
Gregory the Great, Moralia in Iob *31.45.87–90*

Snorting, stamping, affronted by the bit,
Wheeling this way and that as if resenting
Its freedom denied, and swelling with fury
At the pressure of the reins.

And so the up-blown virago
Parades before both lines of troops—
Until she rides up to a single contingent,
Small, with a pauper's weaponry, a ragtag

HUMILITY

Recruited for the war by HUMBLE MIND.
Though royal, HUMBLE MIND is diffident
About her own resources and seeks support

HOPE

From another. For this, she has turned to HOPE,
Whose riches lie beyond the earth,
On high in the wealthy Kingdom.

"Lay not up for yourselves treasures on earth, where rust and worms corrupt and where thieves break through and steal. But lay up for yourselves treasures in heaven. . . ."
Matthew 6:19–20

On seeing HUMBLE MIND, her lack of pomp,
Her paltry arms, PRIDE throws herself
Into a fierce harangue:

THE INVECTIVE OF PRIDE

"Contemptible creatures, are you lost to shame?
With such rabble as *this* would you confront
The captains of the earth, the mighty lords

"Sins are all Lords and great ones."
John Bunyan, The Pilgrim's Progress

Whose virtue in war has won them
Honor and position, ancestral wealth,
And the rich grasslands of empire
To tread beneath their feet?
And is some upstart,
Some stranger without a stitch of clothes,
Now to dispossess those ancient kings?
It is sacrilege to speak it!

"I was a stranger and you took me not in, naked and you clothed me not. . . ."
Matthew 25:43

"Heaven and earth!—of what are you thinking? Are the shades of Pemberley to be thus polluted?"
Jane Austen, Pride and Prejudice, *vol. 3, chap. 14*

"Look at *you* who would wield *our* scepters!
Look at *you* who would plow *our* fields!
Yet you dare challenge our priority
And claim the ground that *we* have cultivated
From the beginning of things.
"Absurd presumption!
From the moment of birth,
When the body is still hot
With the heat of the mother's womb,
The human being belongs to *us*.
We spread our force throughout the new-formed child,
We take up seats of power in its bones.
What space in our realm was ever granted *you*?

ORIGINAL SIN

"And proud Lucifera men did her call,
That made her selfe a Queene, . . .
Yet rightfull kingdome she had none at all,
Ne heritage of native soveraintie,
But did usurpe with wrong and tyrannie
Upon the scepter, which she now did hold."
Edmund Spenser, The Faerie Queene 1.4.12

ADAM

The house and we, its masters,
The child and our sovereign rule,
Are born together on the selfsame day
And grow to an equal strength across the years.

"It has been so ever since the new formation,
ADAM, escaped the bounds of Paradise
To enter a wider world.
Then the man began to clothe himself in skins, *Genesis 3:21*
Naked before, and naked still
Had he not been bent to our command.

"But these new rivals of ours,
These refugees from who knows where,
This wretched, degenerate spawn of no one,
This worthless, indolent, beggarly mass—

"What fairytales must they be trusting
To give their misery such hope,
To console their idleness with expectation!
But idle hope is no consolation in war
To weaklings the warcry never stirs.

Pride assails the Virtues. *London, from the British Library Collection, Cotton MS Cleopatra C VIII, f. 15v*

A chilly virtue fails the feeble soul.
What use is icy CHASTITY in battle?
Imagine milady PIETY in a sweat!

"O ancient God of War,
Where is the honor in facing such opponents,
In trading swordthrusts with these featherweights,
In bearing arms against a dancehall of girls?

"Look at JUSTICE there, who is always needy,
Or INTEGRITY, who is always poor.
Look at pasty-faced ABSTINENCE,
Bonedry SOBRIETY,
And PURITY with blood as pale as milk.
Over there is SIMPLICITY, ever exposed
To any wound or injury,
And here, cringing as always, HUMBLE MIND,
Craven, unfree, even in her own eyes.

"I will have this spineless mob, like stubble,
Trodden under foot. No swords, no spears!
To stain good weapons with their frigid blood
Is unworthy of ancient heroes."

Then Pride sets spur to horse,
Meaning to ride down her enemy,
Overwhelm her with the weight of the charge
And the impact of the horse's shield-hard chest,
Then crush her beneath the churning hooves.
Maddened, she gallops forward
straight into a pit,

THE PIT OF GUILE

A hidden pit that Guile has dug in secret
Across the plain, shrewd Guile,
Shifty artisan of lies
And one of the detestable plague of Sins.
Anticipating war, she gouged the field
With a line of trenches, deep, meant to ensnare,
To swallow up the ranks of enemy troops
As they advanced. She set her camouflage
With branches laid across the opening
And turf to simulate level ground.

By holding her position, Humble Mind
Avoids the murderous device.
But Pride charges blind in her attack,
Riding hard in wild career;
She stumbles at the sudden unseen edge,

"Pride goeth before destruction, and the spirit is lifted up before a fall."
Proverbs 16:18

The pit of Guile and the downfall of Pride. *St. Gallen, Stiftsbibliothek, Cod. Sang. 135, p. 400 (www.e-codices.ch/en/csg/0135/400)*

A chasm opens, and she falls
Headlong into the trap.
Flung forward, she clutches at her horse's neck
But is caught under its weight and pinned.
She writhes among its broken, flailing limbs.

Seeing this monster of vanity crushed
And at the point of death, the quiet Virtue
Makes her way slowly, lifting her face
A modest fraction, pulling in her joy
Behind a kindly look.
She hesitates, but as she hesitates,
Hope is at her side,
Holding out to her an avenging sword,
Breathing into her the love of glory,
And pointing her forward.
Humble Mind grabs Pride by the hair,
Drags her from the pit, and with her left hand
Tilts back the face, bends back the neck,
Then with a stroke cuts head from body
And holds the head high by its blood-wet curls.

The Inspiration of Hope

"And when she had drawn [the sword] out, she took him by the hair of his head . . . and she struck twice upon his neck, and cut off his head, . . . and rolled away his headless body."
Judith 13:9-10

"[N]othing could suggest more vividly the smirk of a persevering governess who has finally succeeded in getting a small boy into trouble with his father."
C. S. Lewis, The Allegory of Love, *chap. 2.*

"God, Creator and Physician of all, knowing that pride is the cause and fountainhead of evil, saw to it that contraries would be healed by contraries, that what had fallen through pride would rise again through humility."
John Cassian, De Institutionibus Coenobiorum et De Octo Principalium Vitiorum Remediis *12.8*

HOPE speaks to PRIDE in death:

"Here end your boasts.
Know that God will break all arrogance.
Know that great things will topple and fall.
Know that everything high will be brought low,
That things puffed up will be punctured.
So put aside your self-importance and beware
The abyss that opens before your feet,
All you high and mighty.
CHRIST tells us often that the lowly are exalted
And the lordly abased.

"And many that are first shall be last: and the last shall be first."
Matthew 19:30; see also 20:16, Mark 10:31, Luke 13:30

"And whosoever shall exalt himself shall be abased, and he that shall humble himself shall be exalted."
Matthew 23:12; see also Luke 14:11 and 20:46

GOLIATH

1 Samuel 17

"We have seen how great GOLIATH fell,
Fearsome in his body, fierce in his rage,
At the hands of a boy with a pebble,
Nothing more,
But it shot through the air from a sling
And punched a hole deep in his forehead.
Brutal, unyielding, swaggering, wild,
Swelling without limit, raging without cease,
Taunting the very air with his great shield,
He learned what a child's toy can do,
This grim man of battle brought down by a boy.

"Fearsome, prodigious, giant, deformed, a void where his eye had been."
Virgil, Aeneid *3.658, on the blinded Cyclops.*

"And from that day I led that boy
As he ripened into manhood.
As his virtue came to flower,
He raised it up and stretched it toward my realm.
For at the feet of the Lord Almighty
Is my immortal home, and when I summon
Those who have triumphed over Sin,
They reach out to me and take hold."

THE ASCENT OF HOPE TO HEAVEN

Then, beating the air with spangled wings,
She takes herself aloft. The Virtues
Marvel at her going; their hearts lift
In longing to go with her.
                                                  But they turn
Back to the strife on earth, the war with Sin,
And ready themselves for their own rewards.

Hope ascends to heaven. *London, from the British Library Collection, Cotton MS Cleopatra C VIII, f. 17v*

The Virtues marvel at the ascent of Hope. *London, from the British Library Collection, Cotton MS Titus D XIV, f. 16r*

FIFTH COMBAT

Riotous Living at her feast. *London, from the British Library Collection, Cotton MS Cleopatra C VIII, f. 18r*

Fifth Combat

FROM THE TWILIT EDGE OF THE EARTH,
From the western lands of the setting sun,
RIOTOUS LIVING has come to the war—

Hair slicked, eyes adrift, speech a lazy drawl;
Long debauched and long past caring,
Lost in a haze of delight.
Pleasure is her raison d'être:
To wallow in sensation,
Weaken her hipshot mind,
Unstring her wits completely.

Even then she was belching up
Remains of an all-night carouse,
For dawn had found her still at a feast
When the call of the bugle came.
Then, slowly she pushed back her cup and arose,
Trampling on fallen flowers,

RIOTOUS LIVING

"Not many days after, the younger son gathered all together and went abroad into a far country, and there wasted his substance, living riotously."
Luke 15:13

Terms also of literary self-indulgence: "Brutus criticized Cicero's style as 'hipshot and unstrung'" (*Tacitus,* Dialogus de Oratoribus *18*).

"Riotous living (LUXURIA) *is the immoderate desire for, or even the love of, partying."*
Spinoza, Ethica *3, "*Affectuum Definitiones*" 45.*

In the moral geography of the classical world, the locus of sensual extravagance was usually imagined as the East, and commentators have had different views of the reversal here. Certainly, Riotous Living is dissociated from the home of Christianity in the eastern Mediterranean, but beyond that, matters are not clear. Perhaps she is to be connected with a decadent Rome in Italy (i.e., in Hesperia, "Land of Evening"); perhaps with Prudentius' homeland of Spain in the far western Mediterranean; perhaps with a Satanic dominion of darkness posited for the western shadows; or perhaps, less precisely but more simply, with the "far country" that is the destination of the prodigal son (Luke 15:13). The issue may be further complicated by the use of "evening" below in reference to the era of the Christian dispensation.

The chariot of Riotous Living. *London, from the British Library Collection, Add MS 24199, f. 18r*

Slipping in puddles of wine
As she stumbled her way to war.
But not a mere foot soldier, she:
When she made her entrance onto the field,
It was in a sumptuous chariot
To wound and win the hearts of awestruck heroes.

And then—a brave new world of warfare.

Not an arrow flies from her bowstring,
Not a spear arcs from her hand,
She brandishes no sword.
Instead she pelts her enemy with roses,
Bombards them with violets,
Assaults their ranks with basket after basket
Of aromatic flowers.

The Virtues are enrapt; the heady scent
Suffuses their bones with sweet, corrosive poison,
Masters their hearts and limbs,
And they forget their strength.
Their spirits fail, defeat is in the air.
They put aside their spears, let fall their hands,
And gawk in shameful admiration

The troops in thrall to Riotous Living. *London, from the British Library Collection, Add MS 24199, f. 18r*

At the lush appointments of the chariot
RIOTOUS LIVING drives.
They marvel at the play of light
On its gem-encrusted sides,
The luster of its gilded reins,
The gold of its solid, massive axle,
The wheels arrayed with silver spokes
And wheelrims of the finest pale electrum.

"... the chariot [of the Sun], Vulcan's work: its axle was of gold, its shaft of gold, its wheelrims of gold, its spokes of silver. Rows of chrysolites and gemstones on its yoke reflected the dazzling light of the Sun himself.... Phaethon [wayward child of the Sun] stared at the craftsmanship and marveled...."
Ovid, Metamorphoses 2.106–13

"That's the ermine white, seventeen coats, hand tinted.... Power steering, power windows, power brakes, power mirrors.... The standard that sets the standard.... I see you're admiring the seats. That's pigskin and *calfskin, hand rubbed."*
Paul Attanasio, Quiz Show

And now the troops are taken
By a longing to surrender,
To abandon their colors uncompelled
And become the willing slaves of RIOTOUS LIVING,
Embracing the rule of this slut of a mistress
And the bylaws of her honkytonk regime.

SOBRIETY

SOBRIETY sees the outrage
Of her comrades deserting the field,
Soldiers never bested in combat
Giving way without a drop of blood,
And she grieves, this stalwart Virtue,
She grieves, but she does not falter.
She plants her standard where all can see,
A great *tau* cross, which she herself has carried
In the forefront of the battle;

"Restore," here Latin INSTAURARE, *punning on Greek* STAUROS, *"cross."*

And by this cross she upbraids the fighters
To restore their unstrung spirits
And make them taut again:

THE EXHORTATION OF SOBRIETY

"Where, where will your madness lead?"
Horace, Epodes 7.1

"Where will your madness lead? Why this sudden strife?"
Virgil, Aeneid 12.313

"Where will your madness lead? Return to your own homes. Where will your madness lead, Danaans?"
Ovid, Heroides 13.130–31

"Where will your madness lead? Can anyone hope to outfox fate?"
Ovid, Metamorphoses 9.429–30

"Ancient and noble house, where will your madness lead? You must never trust this enemy."
Ovid, Fasti 2.225

"What is this frenzy
That has so blinded you?
Where will your madness lead?
Will you have your muscled arms
Bound by ropes of lilies?
Your hands that were meant to wage war
Manacled by fragile flowers?
Will you have your manly hair
Chained up in a golden snood?
And will the brows that once received the mark
Of the King's own holy chrism
Need a pretty saffron headband to contain
The sea of scented oils you pour on?

"Will you sashay? Will your train sweep the floor?
Will you wear silk robes on your delicate frame,
Forsaking the deathless cloth
Woven by TRUE FAITH herself?
And in those silks will you tramp off to feasts
That last throughout the night? And will there be
Deep bowls of foaming wine

"What is this strange frenzy? Where, where do you mean to go?"
Virgil, Aeneid 5.670

"What is this frenzy that has struck your wits like thunder?"
Ovid, Metamorphoses 3.351–52

"What was this frenzy, citizens? What was this tumult of swords?"
Lucan, Bellum Civile 1.8

"What is this frenzy, Phoebus, where Romans trade … blows in a war without enemies?"
Lucan, Bellum Civile 1.681

"What is this frenzy of evil?"
Lucan, Bellum Civile 7.95

"What tumult is there in this monster? What is this frenzy?"
Statius, Thebaid, 2.212–13

"What is this frenzy? Why is the Fury reborn in our domain?"
Statius, Thebaid, 11.329

Sobriety exhorts the backsliding troops. *London, from the British Library Collection, Cotton MS Titus D XIV, f. 17v*

Sloshing and spilling torrents on the tables?
And will the couches be drenched,
And will their cushions be soaked,
And will their coverings still drip
With yesterday's flood?

"Have you forgotten the thirst
Your fathers suffered in the wilderness,
Forgotten the waters leaping from the stone
Split by the mystic staff?
Have you forgotten the manna of heaven
That filled your fathers' tents
In those early days of the world,
Angelic food that in these later times
Of the world's evening
A happier people eats from the body of CHRIST?
And after feasts like these, will you allow
Mere DRUNKENNESS to drag you off
To the dank stews of RIOTOUS LIVING?
When the fury of IDOLATRY and WRATH
Could not force you to yield in open battle,
Will you now sway like a reed in the wind
At the whim of a wine-drenched dancer?

Following the exodus from Egypt, Moses struck a rock with the staff he had earlier used to strike the Nile, and a miraculous fountain issued forth (Exodus 17:1–7, Numbers 20:11). 1 Corinthians 10:4 identifies the rock with Christ.

Exodus 16:14–16

“Stand firm, I implore you all.
Remember who you are, remember CHRIST,
Remember your kindred, your glory,
Your God and King, your Lord.

JUDAH

You are the stock of JUDAH; your noble line
Reaches to the mother of God,
Through whom God became man.

Judah, great-grandson of Abraham, was an ancestor of David and of Joseph, husband of Mary, according to the genealogy set out in Matthew 1.

DAVID

Take inspiration from the glory of DAVID,
Schooled in continual war,

SAMUEL

And from the resolve of SAMUEL,
Who would not touch the spoils of battle
Won from a rich adversary
And did not suffer their heathen king
To live past his defeat and so to threaten
The resumption of war.
He took it as a sin to spare the king,
Even conquered and held captive.
But *you*—you *will* your own captivity.

Obeying the command of God, the prophet Samuel placed the property of the Amalekites under a ban and executed their king despite the reluctance of King Saul (1 Samuel 15); the biblical account, however, raises no ulterior consideration of policy for Samuel's action, such as is offered here. The consequent rift with Saul led directly to Samuel's anointing the young David as rightful king.

Reversing the moral injunction of Aeneas' father, Anchises: "Roman, remember … to spare the conquered and beat down the proud" (Virgil, Aeneid *6.851–53).*

“If you have any fear of God, repent.
Repent your will to follow this sweet Sin,
Repent your foul betrayal.

Repent, and there is no lasting harm.
Know that JONATHAN repented of the honey
He had gathered on the tip of his staff
And tasted, violating a solemn fast;
And the will to kingship charmed the boy,
And he betrayed his oaths.
But because he then repented, he was spared
The pitiless sentence of his father's ax.

THE REPENTANCE OF JONATHAN

Unaware that his father, Saul, had decreed a fast for the day of battle, Jonathan tasted some honey he discovered in a forest. When informed of the decree, he criticized his father, perhaps treasonously implying that his own reign would be superior. He later admitted violating the fast but was saved from execution by acclamation of the people for his heroism in the war (1 Samuel 14:24–46). Repentance actually plays little role in the biblical narrative, but the episode is silently assimilated here to the parable of the prodigal son in Luke 15, an account of a wayward child in which repentance is, of course, key.

"First to assume the consulship and its pitiless ax [of office], this father will condemn his sons for stirring up war again. . . ."
Virgil, Aeneid *6.819-21, on Brutus, first consul of the Roman Republic, who had his children executed for rebellion against the infant state*

"Join with me now and—see!—
I, SOBRIETY, will open the way
For all the Virtues to follow.
Let RIOTOUS LIVING pay for her seductions;
Let her and her subordinates all pay
Under the judgment of CHRIST."

Then SOBRIETY sets the cross of the Lord
In the face of the chariot horses,
Thrusting the venerable wood
Hard up against their bridles.
The horses start in terror at the flash
Of its high brow and outspread horns,
And they bolt, running headlong, heedless,
Hurtling down a sharp incline.

"Horns" (Latin CORNUA*) is a common metaphor for the "arms" of a cross. Less sure is the source or even the nature of the cross's flash. Several commentators have imagined a glitter of gems or precious metals along the top of the cross, while a tenth-century manuscript now in Brussels depicts the cross being wielded as a weapon belching flames (see p. 73.) But the word rendered here as "flash" (Latin* CORUSCUM*) may also refer to a shaking or brandishing motion.*

Already figured by the wooden staffs of Moses and Jonathan, the cross is now described in literal terms appropriate to the supernatural bull (Latin TAURUS*; cf. Greek* STAUROS*, "cross") with eyes of fire whose appearance panicked the horses of Hippolytus, causing his death by dragging, the literary pattern for the downfall of Riotous Living here. In Ovid's version, the restored Hippolytus narrates his own destruction:*

(continued on p. 74)

Sobriety wielding the cross. *Brussels, KBR Ms. 10066–77, f. 126r*

And leaning far back, all her weight on the reins,
Their charioteer hurtles with them,
Her glistening hair now fouled and caked
With dust as she is thrown,
Then dragged, then caught up in the wheels,
Pitched forward and wedged under the axle,
Her fallen body becoming the brake
That finally brings the chariot to a stop.

THE DOWNFALL OF RIOTOUS LIVING

SOBRIETY strikes the deathblow.
Prying a hefty stone from the rockface—
For she carries no weapons at all,
Nothing but the standard of the cross—
She hurls it at RIOTOUS LIVING and hits home,
Staving in the center of her face.
The nose is shattered, lips are driven hard
Into the cavity that was a mouth.
Uprooted teeth and shreds of tongue,
Pulped bits of her own flesh are forced
Down into her own throat.
Her gorge rises at such a meal,
Spewing up her blood, her bones,
And swallowing in turn.

THE DEADLY EUCHARIST

(*continued from p. 37*)
"My horses hurtled down steep rocks.... Leaning far back, I pulled hard on the reins .... I was thrown ..., dragged along ..., part of me ripped away, part still stuck on a tree stump ..., my body all one wound." (Metamorphoses 15.517–29)

Prudentius presents a version of the scene in his account of the Roman martyr Hippolytus at Peristephanon *11.85ff.*

The overthrow of Riotous Living. *London, from the British Library Collection, Cotton MS Cleopatra C VIII, f. 21v*

The girl looks down at her:
"Drink up!
So many cups of wine, now your own blood;
So many suppers, now a grim dessert,
The acid taste of death
In this last, shuddering gulp."

THE TROOPS OF RIOTOUS LIVING ROUTED

The Vice now dead,
Her troops all flit away in fright.
FLIPPANCY and PLAY both drop their toys
And run, the tinkling cymbals they brought to war,
Thinking such rattles would do as weapons.
DESIRE too turns tail, abandoning
His bow and arrows on the field.
PARADE runs off without her splendid gown,
And GLAMOR loses her accessories,
Her gold tiara, necklace, garlands, jewels,
Disordered, torn, and left behind.
Even PLEASURE herself,
Running down through the briars
And across through the brambles,
Does not stop to complain about the thorns
That rip into her calves and lacerate
Her soft, white, pretty feet,
Such is her terror.

"Ah, never let the sharp ice cut your soft, white, pretty feet!"
Virgil, Eclogues 10.49

All along the headlong rout
Lies a trail of cast-off objects—
Hairpins, ribbons, headbands, veils, a brooch,
A diadem, a collar, bodystays—
Spoils that SOBRIETY's men do not pick up
But, keeping their eyes from the joys of plunder,
Grind beneath their calloused heels instead.

Pleasure in full flight. *London, from the British Library Collection, Add MS 24199, f. 22r*

SIXTH COMBAT

Greed. *London, from the British Library Collection, Cotton MS Titus D XVI, f. 20v*

Sixth Combat

Greed

THEY SAY THAT IT WAS GREED WHO CARRIED OFF
The goods RIOTOUS LIVING left behind,
Scrabbling at the dirt with hooklike hands
For any fallen bit of gold
And leering at each piece before loading it
Into the cavernous folds of her gown.

"When did the folds of Greed's gown ever gape wider than now?"
Juvenal, Satires *1.87–88*

But filling these is not enough. She stuffs
Sacks, purses, moneybags to bursting,
Hiding them all with her left hand
Under cover of her cloak
While her right hand scrapes the ground for more.

"Lies Anger Corruption Incompetence Chaos Decay"
The New York Times Sunday Review, *Early Edition, October 18, 2020, p. 1*

FAITHLESSNESS, HUNGER, ANXIETY, DREAD,
PERJURY, FRAUD, DELUSION,
TERROR, ANGUISH, SLEEPLESSNESS,
CORRUPTION, DEFILEMENT, RUIN—

"Every sin has its army against us. . . . From greed there spring faithlessness, fraud, deceit, perjury, sleeplessness, violence, and hardness of heart against compassion."
Gregory the Great, Moralia in Iob, *31.45.88*

"May you be damned, you ancient wolf, who have more prey than any beast to feed your bottomless hunger."
Dante, Purgatorio 20.10–12

"Accursed hunger for gold, to what do you not drive the hearts of men?"
Virgil, Aeneid 3.56–57 *and Dante,* Purgatorio 22.40–41

"And then there followed a lesser age, and with it came battle madness and lust for gain."
Virgil, Aeneid 8.326–27

These are all attendants of Greed
And they run with the Crimes, Greed's children,
Reared on their mother's inkblack milk,
Now prowling the field like wolves.

Thus a soldier kills his brother for a helmet
Studded with tawny gemstones;
Another finds his father among the fallen
And strips the splendid armor from his corpse.
Civil War makes plunder out of kin,
Lust for Gain spares not even his own,
Hunger despoils her children.
And this is how
Greed lets loose her slaughter on the world,
Laying a hundred thousand low
In a hundred thousand ways of wounding.
One man she blinds by forcing out his eyes
And sends him stumbling through the dark

"First the lust for money, then for power, became rife, and these became the seeds of other evils. For greed destroyed faith, integrity, and every other noble quality; and in their place, it taught pride, cruelty, neglect of the gods, and the commodification of all things. . . . Steeped as it were in evil toxins, it makes a man womanish in body and mind. It is limitless, insatiable; neither want nor plenty ever make it less."
Sallust, Bellum Catilinae 10–11

"From greed proceed anger, . . . lust, . . . loss of judgment, deception, pride, . . . malice, . . . vindictiveness, shamelessness, loss of prosperity, loss of virtue, anxiety, . . . infamy, . . . pitilessness, . . . malevolence, . . . mistrust, . . . insincerity towards all, appropriation of other people's wealth, ravishment of other people's wives, harshness of speech, . . . propensity to speak ill of others, . . . gluttony, liability to premature death, . . . irresistible liking for falsehood, . . . insatiable desire for indulging the ear, evil-speaking, boastfulness, . . . neglect of duties, rashness, and perpetration of every kind of evil act."
Mahabharata, 12.158

"The love of money is the root of all evils."
1 Timothy 6:10

Greed cheats the sight of men. *Paris, BnF Ms. lat. 15158, f. 51r*

Greed drives men toward open fires. *Paris, BnF Ms. lat. 15158, f. 51r*

"The Church says Covetousness is a deadly sin—but does she really think so? Is she ready to found Welfare Societies to deal with financial immorality as she does with sexual immorality? Do the officials stationed at church doors in Italy to exclude women with bare arms turn anybody away on the grounds that they are too well dressed to be honest? . . . Is Dives, like Magdalen, ever refused the sacraments on the grounds that he, like her, is an 'open and notorious evil-liver'? Does the Church arrange services with bright congregational singing for Total Abstainers from Usury?"
Dorothy L. Sayers, The Other Six Deadly Sins

Without even a staff to keep him straight.
A second she forces to see, yet cheats his sight
With some beguiling object;
He reaches for it and is caught,
Her knife blade swift and silent in his heart.
And others, many others, she drives headlong
Toward open fires of furnaces so hot
That the gold within is burning,
And he who would take what is not his own
Must likewise burn to get it.

She pounces on the whole of humankind,
Surprising all mortality with ruin—
No more furious Vice than GREED
To ensnare the world's people
In earthly disaster and the flames of Hell.

And now, at the limit of her daring,
She begins to move against the priests of God,
Leaders in the foremost ranks,
Who fill their trumpets with a thunderous sound.
But REASON in her armor shelters them
From the brunt of the attack;

"The root of all evil is greed, that is to say, wanting more than is enough. . . ."
Augustine, De Libero Arbitrio *3.17.48.165–66*

Reading PECULATOR*, "embezzler," with the oldest manuscript.*

The ancient Israelite priesthood was first consecrated when members of the tribe of Levi stood with Moses at Sinai against the worshippers of the golden calf (Exodus 32) in what itself may have been read as an allegory of priestly proof against greed. Leading the people with the blowing of trumpets was among the original duties of the priests (Numbers 10:1–10), notably fulfilled at the siege of Jericho (Joshua 6), referenced below.

REASON SHIELDS THE LEVITICAL PRIESTHOOD

Ever the friend of LEVI's people,
She stretches out her shield to keep them safe.
With the good work of REASON, they stand firm,
Secure amid the violence; only a few
Sustain any wounds at all,
And these no more than scratches.

"Good work of Reason," reflecting Latin RATIONIS OPE, *linked anagrammatically with* OPERATIO, *Good Works, Reason's ally against Greed below.*

Appalled at the failure of her onslaught,
GREED cries out in fury:
"Am I losing then?
My ancient force is blunted, the savage power
Faded now that once could breach
The hearts of human beings without distinction.
No nature so tough, so ironbound,
It long stayed deaf to the clink of copper coins
Or insensitive to gold.
Every character, every sort,
Every condition of man fell before me—
The hard, the bitter, the tenderhearted,
The scholar and the simpleton,
The scrupulous, the moral idiot—
All sent down to Death by my right hand.
Whatever the grasping Styx guards by its banks
Is mine and mine alone. The treasure house

THE SOLILOQUY OF GREED

Contrast the discovery of Dante: "Master, tell me, who are these people? And those on the left, the tonsured ones, were they all clergy?" . . . "Those without hair on their heads were priests and popes and cardinals. In them greed reaches its greatest height." (Inferno 7.37–39, 46–48)

"My powers are exhausted, glutted now with hate."
Juno, at Virgil, Aeneid 7.297–98

Reason shields the priesthood from Greed. *St. Gallen, Stiftsbibliothek, Cod. Sang. 135, p. 420 (www.e-codices.ch/en/csg/0135/420)*

Of Tartarus owes all its hoard to me.
Mine are the dreams of the world's generations,
Mine the world's toiling, its mad striving mine.

"How comes it that such power has collapsed?
That Fortune makes a mockery of my strength?
The image on a gold or silver coin
Means nothing to CHRIST's people; wealth,
All wealth, is rust and tarnish in their eyes.
Where did they learn this strange discrimination?

JUDAH ISCARIOT

"Did I not triumph over ISCARIOT,
Great among the disciples of their God
And intimate enough to share his supper,
Who dipped his hand in the selfsame dish *Matthew 26:23*
Yet still meant to betray him?
He fell with a fevered lust upon a weapon
That *I* wielded, and having bought a field
With the blood of his God and friend,
He paid with a twisted neck for his betrayal. *Matthew 27:5*

"I triumphed too at Jericho
Even as the city faced its end;
For, flush with victory

Greed the deceiver. *Lyon, Bibliothèque de la Part-Dieu, P. A. 22, f. 9r (photo: IRHT-CNRS)*

Greed disguises herself. *Lyon, Bibliothèque de la Part-Dieu, P. A. 22, f. 8v* (*photo: IRHT-CNRS*)

Achar

Amid the ruin of those great walls,
ACHAR succumbed to the lure of gold
Looted from the smoldering town.
A glittering thing he found among the ashes,
But a thing forbidden and accursed.
And the distinction of his family did not save him,
Nor his descent from JUDAH, patriarch
Blessed in the lineage of CHRIST.
Let those who take this people as their pattern
Accept the form of this destruction:
Where there is one people, let there be
A single price to pay.
"But now, to work—

After the fall of Jericho, Achar, a soldier of the tribe of Judah, violated a holy ban against plunder, for which he was executed by stoning, all his children and his goods condemned to be burnt (Joshua 7). Dante cites him as an exemplar of greed at Purgatorio 20.109–11.

Aaron of the tribe of Levi was the brother of Moses and the first high priest.

"Since I cannot match the countrymen of JUDAH
Or the high priest AARON in open war,
Then let me find some stratagem to catch them.
Victory through arms or through deceit
Is victory all the same."
And with these words,
She drops her weapons,
Sloughs off her grim appearance,
And shifts her shape,

"If I cannot sway the gods above, I will rouse the world below."
Juno, at Virgil, Aeneid 7.312

"Deceit or valor—in war who asks?"
Virgil, Aeneid 2.390

Greed masquerades as Economy

"The Fury sloughed off her grim appearance and shifted her shape, becoming an old woman."
Virgil, Aeneid 7.415–16

Becoming in semblance and demeanor
The reputable Virtue called ECONOMY.
This is the Virtue of the thrifty life,
Careful for what is her own;
And as this Virtue-in-facsimile,
GREED does not grasp or claw
But comports herself as a frugal thing,
Setting a matron's mantle on her head
To cover hair alive with writhing snakes,
Veiling herself with a thin white cloth
To hide the madness beneath,
The lurking fury.
Avarice, hoarding, rapine, theft—
all masked
As a mother's concern for her children.

Some men are taken in,
Captives of their credulity,
And they follow this unholy Erinys
Convinced she does a Virtue's work.
The leaders are confounded,
Their companies perplexed,
And the front line begins to falter,

"Greed is a deceptive vice with the guise and appearance of virtue, stern in its bearing and austere in its looks. Certainly the miser is praised as 'frugal' and 'thrifty,' as he watches out over his own. . . ."
Juvenal, Satires 14.109–12

The fifth-century Indian scholar Bhadantacariya Buddhaghosi developed the ethical concept of the "near enemy," the vice whose structural likeness to a virtue is such that the two may easily be confused, as we could say dependency may be confused with love, or indifference with the virtue of detachment. The near enemy poses a special moral threat "since it is able to corrupt owing to its similarity, like an enemy masquerading as a friend." In his analysis, greed is the near enemy not of economy, but of loving-kindness "since both share in seeing merits" in things outside the self. (Paramatthamañjusa, 309; Visuddhimagga 9.98)

"The huge serpent . . . entwines itself into her hair, slinks into her limbs. As the poison first pervades her senses . . . but does not yet overwhelm her soul . . . she speaks softly in the usual tones of motherhood."
Virgil, Aeneid 7.352–57, *on the Fury's attack on Amata*

"Greed often exhorts the conquered mind as if with reason when it says, 'There is no harm in your wanting some things to possess, because you do not seek to be increased by them, but are only afraid of being in want; and what someone else keeps for no real good, you yourself will use for a better purpose.'"
Gregory the Great, Moralia in Iob 31.45.90

The Virtues' army wavers in doubt. *Lyon, Bibliothèque de la Part-Dieu, P. A. 22, f. 9v* (*photo: IRHT-CNRS*)

Wavering in doubt about this creature
Of two forms, where in her to see a friend
And where an enemy. Her fluid shape,
Ambiguous and deadly,
Erodes the old stability of their sight.

Things happen quickly now.
With a shout
THE GOOD WORKS OF BENEVOLENCE
Comes bounding to the middle of the field,
Surging forward from the rearmost ranks
In aid of her companions,
The final Virtue to engage but singly capable
Of letting no sadness abide.
Sudden, swift, and light,
She has stripped every burden from her shoulders,
Once weighed down with wealth
Now freed through her kindness to the poor.
Openhanded with her fortune,
Giving with a sound prodigality,
She is rich with the treasures of TRUE FAITH,
Seeing her empty purse, yet reckoning up
The sum of her wealth in heaven.

OPENHANDEDNESS

Latin OPERATIO, *punning on* OPERE RATIO, *"Reason in practice" or "Reason via works."*

"It is characteristic of the openhanded even to go to excess in giving, leaving too little for themselves; for it is typical of them to ignore their own interests."
Aristotle, Nicomachean Ethics *1120b5*

"For at least another hundred years we must pretend to ourselves . . . that fair is foul and foul is fair; for foul is useful and fair is not. Avarice and usury . . . must be our gods for a little longer still."
John Maynard Keynes, Essays in Persuasion, *chap. 5*

"The young man saith to him: 'All these [commandments] have I kept from my youth, what is yet wanting to me?' Jesus saith to him: 'If thou wilt be perfect, go sell what thou hast and give to the poor, and thou shalt have treasure in heaven, and come and follow me.' And when the young man heard this, he went away in sadness: for he had great possessions."
Matthew 19:20–22

Her coming is a thunderbolt to GREED,
Who turns cold with terror, unable to move,
Unable to speak,
But sure of her instant death—
No guile left in her to entice
The Virtue who treads the world beneath her feet
Like a countrywoman making wine,
No way to inveigle her again
With the gold she so despised.

Then an iron vise of arms around the throat,
Strangling, wringing out the blood
Till it is dry; and under the chin,
Like bands tightening, choking,
Twisting away all breath, destroying life
Not through an open wound
But with the stoppage of her air,
Death shut within the prisonhouse of her body.

THE DESPOILING OF GREED

GREED struggles, flails,
But there is a foot and a knee on her chest
And spearthrusts through her ribs and groin,
And soon her corpse is stripped of spoils:
Dirty bits of unworked gold,
Untried as yet in fire,

"Gold . . . and everything that may abide the fire . . . shall be purified by fire. . . ."
Numbers 31:22–23

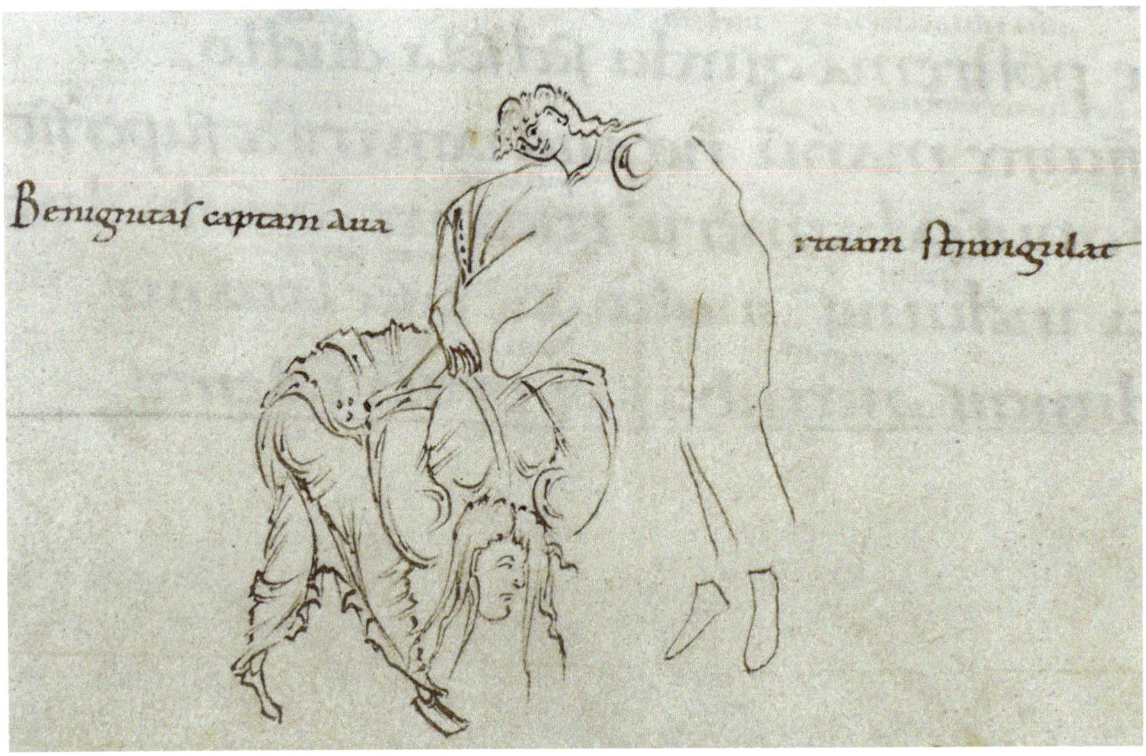

Greed bound and strangled. *London, from the British Library Collection, Add MS 24199, f. 27v*

"Lay not up for yourselves treasures on earth, where rust and worms corrupt. . . ."
Matthew 6:19

Moneybags eaten through with worms,
And bronze coins green with rust,
Things long hoarded, laid away—
All these the triumphant Virtue takes
And distributes to the poor.

"I counsel thee to buy of me gold tried in the fire, that thou mayest be rich."
Revelation 3:18

Then to the encircling thousands:

Openhandedness addresses the troops

"Cast off your armor, righteous souls,
And lay your weapons down,
For the cause of our evil lies dead;
The gluttony for gain is dead,
And the sanctified may rest.
For it is the most perfect rest
To wish for nothing beyond your need—
The simplest food to restore your body,
A single garment to cover you,
And when nature's measure is complete,
Nothing further, nothing more.

"Cast off your fear, you men of Troy, set your anxiety aside."
Virgil, Aeneid 1.562

"Keep no scrip for your journey,
Nor plan for a second coat to wear.
Be not troubled about your sustenance
Tomorrow, if you will have food to eat:

"Do not possess gold nor silver nor money in your purses, nor scrip for your journey, nor two coats, nor shoes, nor a staff. . . . Are not two sparrows sold for a pittance? And not one of them shall fall on the ground without your Father."
Matthew 10:9–10, 10:29

Bread for the day returns with the sun.
Consider the faith of birds, how easy
They are about the day to come,
Trusting they will be fed by God's provision.
The meanest creatures of the air,
Even sparrows sold for a pittance,
Have a sure and certain faith
That their nurture will not fail,
That a great and mighty God
Cares for them, that they may not die.

"And you, who are beloved of God
And the image of CHRIST,
Can you think your Creator will desert you?
O humankind, put aside your fear:
He who gives life gives food.
In heaven's teaching is your food—
Look for it there—the food that brings light,
That nourishes, that strengthens the hope
Of life endless and incorruptible.
And be not mindful of the body,
For *he* is mindful who created it,
And he will furnish it with food
And he will care for its needs."

"Take no thought for your life, what you shall eat ... nor for your body, what you shall wear. Is not life more than meat and the body more than raiment? Behold the birds of the air, for they neither sow, nor do they reap ... yet your heavenly Father feedeth them. And are you not of much more value than they?"
Matthew 6:25–26

THE VIRTUES RETIRE IN TRIUMPH

Peace drives off Dread and Suffering. *Paris, BnF Ms. lat. 15158, f. 55v*

The Virtues Retire in Triumph

AND NOW THEIR FEAR DEPARTS,
And SUFFERING, VIOLENCE, OUTRAGE, DREAD,
And TREACHERY, naysayer of TRUE FAITH,
Are driven from the land.

THE WORK OF PEACE BEGINS

Under the kindly eye of PEACE
Grim WAR is banished and ALARM stands down,
Unbelting his battle gear,
Letting fall the hem of his soldier's kit,
And moderating his military gait
To a stately civilian amble.

Every trumpet is still, every sword
Sleeps in its scabbard.

And the dust of battle is cleared away,
And the sky begins to glow
With a deep, resplendent light.

THE VIRTUES RETIRE IN TRIUMPH

In pagan contexts, always Jupiter, but here with the resonance of such passages as Exodus 19:16: "Behold thunders began to be heard, and lightning to flash, and a very thick cloud to cover the mount. . . ."

And gladly the army sees
The face of the Thundering God
Smiling on them from above,
And in the height
CHRIST rejoicing in the victory
And opening to his servants
The doors of his Father's place
Within the deeps of heaven.

"To him that shall win a victory, I shall give to sit with me on my throne, as I also have won a victory, and am set down with my Father on his throne."
Revelation 3:21

CONCORD

CONCORD signals the return to camp
Under triumphant banners.
Never did an army look so fine,
So glorious, as these troops do now,
Their double columns led in long array,
Footsoldiers in marching order
Bright with song,
A line of horsemen answering them
With resounding hymns of their own.

SIMILE OF THE RED SEA CROSSING

EVEN AS
victorious Israël once sang,
Seeing the chasm of the waters
Open wide behind their backs,
As step by step they set their feet

"Then Moses and the children of Israel sang . . . : 'I will sing to the Lord, for he hath triumphed gloriously: the horse and his rider he hath thrown into the sea. The Lord is my strength and my praise,

(continued on p. 104)

Concord orders a return to camp. *Lyon, Bibliothèque de la Part-Dieu, P. A. 22, f. 18v* (*photo: IRHT-CNRS*)

Victorious troops in song. *London, from the British Library Collection, Cotton MS Cleopatra C VIII, f. 31r*

Commenting on Psalm 113, "When Israel went out of Egypt," which he set in the mouths of souls newly arriving in Purgatory (Purgatorio 2.46), *Dante wrote: "If we look at it in the literal sense, it means the departure of the Children of Israel from Egypt in the time of Moses; if in the allegorical sense, it means our redemption through Christ; if in the moral sense, it means the conversion of the soul from the misery of sin to the state of grace; if in the anagogical sense, it means the leavetaking of the blessed soul from the slavery of this corruption to the freedom of everlasting glory. Although these mystical senses are called by many names, they all can be called 'allegorical' since they are different, or 'other' (in Greek, alleon* [*sic*]), *than the literal"* (Letter to Can Grande, 20–21).

Dry on the further shore
When at their heels
Mountains of water hanging in air
Suddenly came crashing down
To engulf the dark people of the Nile
And sink them in the depths;
And fish returned to swim again
In all the flooded places
Where there had been bare sand.
And the company of God took up their timbrels
And beat them with their beaters
And sang of this wondrous work of God
To be told through the world's generations,
How he split the sea and stilled the wind,
How he lifted banks of water on both sides,
How he held them there suspended
Letting passage for his people on dry land—

JUST SO,
the Virtues' songs ring out this day
In sweet melodious psalms,
For the nation of Sins is at last overcome.

(*continued from p. 102*)
and he is become my salvation: he is my God and I will glorify him, the God of my father and I will exalt him. The Lord is as a man of war, Almighty is his name. Pharaoh's chariots and his army he hath cast into the sea: his chosen captains are drowned in the Red Sea. The depths have covered them, they are sunk to the bottom like a stone. . . .' And Miriam the prophetess, sister of Aaron, took a timbrel in her hand . . . and she began the song . . . : 'Sing to the Lord, for he hath triumphed gloriously: the horse and his rider he hath thrown into the sea.'"
Exodus 15:1–21

The Vices skulk away. *Lyon, Bibliothèque de la Part-Dieu, P. A. 22, f. 15v* (*photo: IRHT-CNRS*)

THE FINAL STRUGGLE

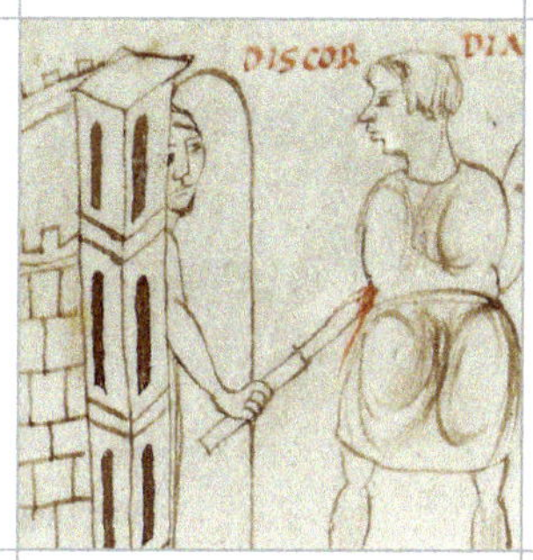

"Our battle is with greed, with lewdness, anger, and ambition.
We have a continual and stubborn fight with the vices of the flesh
and the allurements of the world. Besieged on all sides . . .
the mind of man opposes these enemies one by one. . . .
If greed is laid low, then lust springs up; if lust is overcome,
ambition takes its place. If ambition is put aside,
anger provokes, pride puffs up, drunkenness entices,
and spite destroys concord. . . ."

CYPRIAN OF CARTHAGE, *DE MORTALITATE* 4

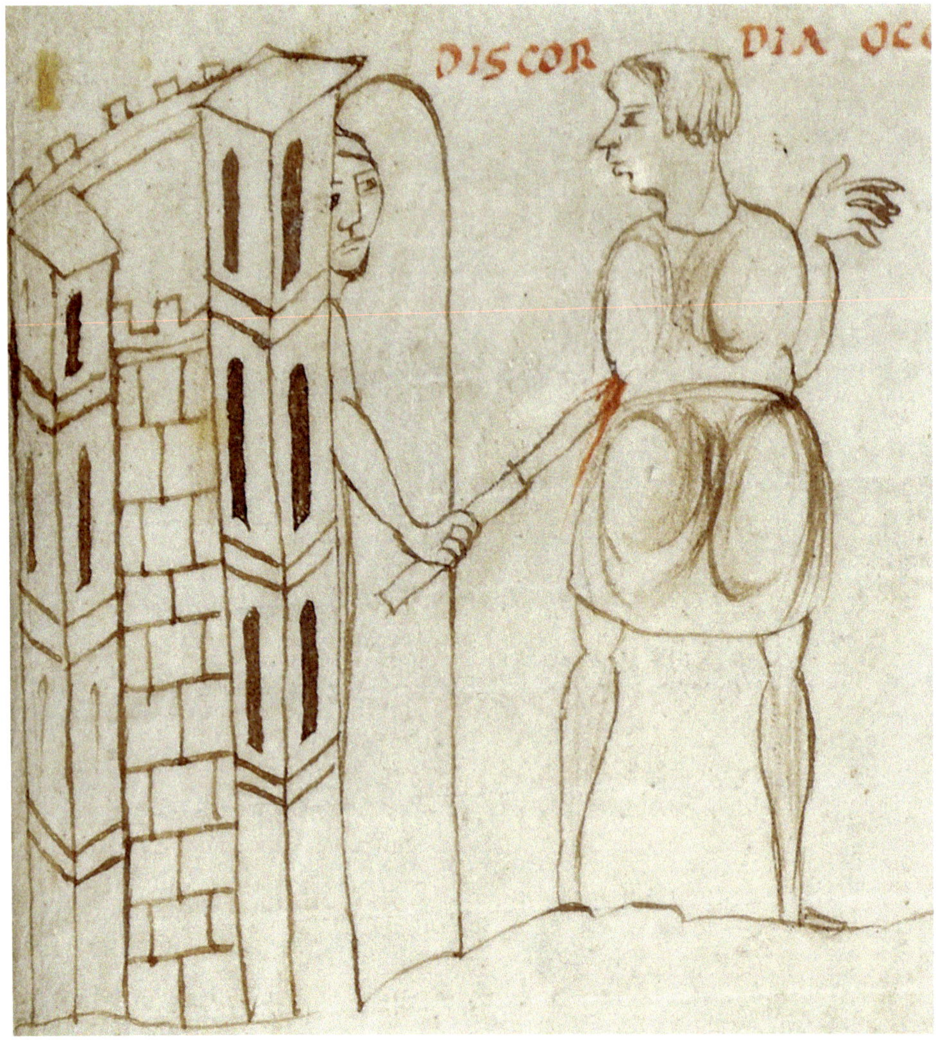

The assault on Concord. *Brussels, KBR Ms. 9987-91, f. 123r*

The Final Struggle

AT THE ENTRANCE TO THE CAMP THE PASSAGE NARROWS
Just by the barrier where a double gate
Swings on its hinges open or shut.
Here a storm breaks unforeseen
To trouble PEACE and spite the victory
With sudden disaster.

"Enter ye in at the narrow gate. . . . How narrow is the gate and strait is the way that leadeth unto life, and few there be that find it."
Matthew 7:13–14

"Strive to enter by the narrow gate; for many . . . shall seek to enter, and shall not be able."
Luke 13:24

For as CONCORD sets foot within the walls,
Close-packed, elbow-to-elbow with the troops
Jostling around her,
A blow comes on her left side,
The swift thrust of a knife
From an enemy hidden in the crowd.
The strength of CONCORD's armor keeps the blade
From penetrating deep—
Row upon row of interlocking links
Bound into a fabric of hard steel
Enveloping her body,
Tough-knotted mesh,

THE ARMOR OF CONCORD

Dense, resilient, stiff—
Yet one loose link
At the end of one row
On the seam between tunic and skirt
Lets the thin point of the knife pass through.

Discord, known too as Heresy

Discord struck that blow,
Cloaked as a friend amid our ranks,
Her own torn robe and Hydra-headed scourge
Left lying with the debris of death
On the field where the Sins met defeat.

"Exultant Discord strode forward, her robe torn, followed by the war goddess with a bloody scourge."
Virgil, Aeneid 8.702–3

And now with an olive wreath on her head
She mouths glad songs of victory
In company with victorious troops
While hidden in her cloak there is a dagger,
Treachery meant for you, greatest of Virtues,
For you, yes, Concord, you.
She does not drive it deep into your body—
That crime is not permitted her—
But she marks the surface of your skin
With a thin, dark scribble of your blood.

Shaken, CONCORD asks:

"What does this mean?
What good does it do to have stilled the Passions
And destroyed the Sins in righteous war
If a Virtue is attacked in time of peace?"

The troops turn their eyes to her,
Alarmed at the blood
They see seeping through her mail,
Red token of the wound beneath.

But they also read the marks of fear
In the assassin standing close,
The trembling hands and sudden pallor
That betray her guilt to everyone.

And at once they are on her, all of them,
Swords drawn, demanding in a roar
Her name, her origins, her country, her beliefs,
The God she worships, and the whereabouts
Of him who sent her here.

Discord wounds Concord. *London, from the British Library Collection, Cotton MS Titus D XVI, f. 26v*

Discord/Heresy discovered. *London, from the British Library Collection, Cotton MS Titus D XVI, f. 28r*

And she:

THE CONFESSION OF HERESY

"I am called DISCORD, surnamed HERESY,
And mine is a disparate, evershifting God.
Now he is lesser, or then again greater;
Now he is double, now single, unalloyed.
When I would have it so, he is mere seeming,
A phantom, God of air;
Or when my fancy is to play with God,
He becomes the soul within me.
BELIAL is my teacher,
My home and country is the world."
No more!
Not another blasphemy from this monster!
TRUE FAITH shuts her up for good
With a spearthrust through her voicebox
And a spike impaling her tongue.
A hundred hands rip HERESY apart,

THE RENDING OF DISCORD

A sardonic conflation of various contemporary theological views at odds with the orthodox position on the Trinity as fixed at the Council of Nicaea in 325 and affirmed at the First Council of Constantinople in 381; in other poems, Prudentius discusses and dismisses them all. One view, most closely associated with the name of Arius (d. 336), held that there is no equality within the Trinity but that the Son is lesser and the Father greater (see Prudentius, Apotheosis *252ff.). The dualism of Marcion (ca. 85 to ca. 160) dissociated the God of the Hebrew Scriptures from the God of the Gospels; the division was later subsumed in the doctrines of Manichaeism (so called after the Persian Mani, d. ca. 276) as a competition between divinities of darkness and light (see Prudentius,* Hamartigenia *Praef. 36ff.). The unitarianism of Sabellius (excommunicated ca. 220) regarded the members of the Trinity as modes of a single person, identified as the Father (see* Apotheosis *178ff.). A teaching known as Docetism held the physical presence of the Son to be an illusion, "a God of air without real body . . . a false phantom and empty likeness of the body, having nothing tangible to it"* (Apotheosis *956–58).* *At* Apotheosis *820ff., Prudentius condemns the pantheistic notion that the soul is "an actual part of God."*

Originally simply a Hebrew term for worthlessness, Belial developed into an important demon in Jewish literature in the Second Temple period. Christian usage will resonate with Paul's question at 2 Corinthians 6:15, "What accord is there between Christ and Belial? Or what part hath the believer with the unbeliever?"

Heresy silenced. *London, from the British Library Collection, Cotton MS Titus D XVI, f. 28v*

The rending of Discord. *London, from the British Library Collection, Cotton MS Titus D XVI, f. 28v*

Scraps of her body flung wide to the wind,
Thrown to dogs or carrion crows,
Sunk in the shitstink of sewers
Or on the seabottom for slimy things
To suck at and devour.
So passes HERESY,
Rawflesh for unclean beasts.

The deaths of actual heresiarchs were similarly moralized by early Church historians, e.g., the death of Arius as related by Socrates of Constantinople: "It was then Saturday, and Arius was expecting to assemble with the church on the day following, but divine retribution overtook his daring criminalities. For going out of the imperial palace, … he paraded proudly through the midst of the city, attracting the notice of all the people. As he approached … Constantine's Forum, … a terror arising from the bite of conscience seized him, and with the terror a violent relaxation of the bowels: he therefore asked whether there was a convenient place near by, and being directed to the back of Constantine's Forum, he hurried there as fast as he could. Soon after, a faintness came over him, and together with the evacuations his bowels protruded, followed by a copious hemorrhage, and the descent of the smaller intestines: moreover portions of his spleen and liver were brought off in the effusion of blood, so that he almost immediately died. The scene of this catastrophe is still shown …; and by passersby pointing their fingers at the place, there is a perpetual memorial of this extraordinary kind of death" (Historia Ecclesiastica 38).

"They all tear at him with their weapons, rip quivering limb from limb.… Some go for his face, pluck out still-living eyes; others run off with the arms they have wrenched from their sockets. Someone cuts off a foot, someone else twists a shoulder away. This one cracks the spine, breaks open the ribcage; that one lays bare the liver, the heart, the lungs that still gasp for air. There is no space for all the anger, no room for all the hate: they barely leave the corpse even well after its death but still hack it to bits with their spears."
Claudian, In Rufinum 2.410–17

CONCORD AND TRUE FAITH

True Faith and Concord in their camp. *Brussels, KBR Ms. 10066-77, f. 134r*

Concord and True Faith

Some manuscripts read here instead:
"After peaceful thoughts can dwell protected
Within the safety of the ramparts
And all disquiet yields to calm. . . ."

THE TRIBUNAL

NOW THAT THE COMMONWEALTH IS SET TO RIGHT
And the moral frame restored,
Now that the thinking of the people at peace
Is safely settled behind the ramparts,
They build a platform on the higher ground
At the center of the camp, a tribunal
Where the earth slopes sharply upward in a rise
Affording a natural vantage, unobstructed
On all sides.
And here, TRUE FAITH and CONCORD,
Sisters in CHRIST's love,
Mount the height together and take their stand,
Equal in their sanctity and honor
And towering above all else.

Then from this place in full view of the people,
They summon the whole camp to assemble.
No part of the Soul lies hidden,
Idle in some unseen crevice

"The building circular—A cage, glazed—a glass lantern . . . —The prisoners in their cells, occupying the circumference—The officers in the center . . . hence the sentiment

(*continued on p. 122*)

Of the body, but every tent is exposed,
Every tentflap drawn back,
Every canvas curtain opened,
And there is no private shirking unobserved.

(*continued from p. 121*)
of a sort of omnipresence—
The whole circuit reviewable with little, or if necessary without any, change of place. One station in the inspection part affording the most perfect view of every cell."
Jeremy Bentham on the Panopticon, Proposal for a New and Less Expensive Mode of Employing and Reforming Convicts

CONCORD begins:

THE SPEECH OF CONCORD

"Children of the Father! Children of CHRIST!

"The barbarians encircling the holy city
Have been destroyed,
And for this you have all won great glory.
But public calm depends on private consensus
In both the city's core and its surroundings;
Domestic schism shakes the commonwealth
And disruption at home means disorder abroad.
So all of you, my soldiers, must ensure
That there be no discordant element
In our thinking, no alien belief
Among us, kindled in secret frictions.
A divided will produces monsters,
Dichotomous creatures hidden
Within hearts at variance.

Visigothic armies under King Alaric ravaged Italy several times during the first decade of the fifth century. Prudentius celebrated a battlefield victory over the invaders in 402 (or 403) in the triumphal voice of Rome herself: "Let all fear be gone! We have overcome and now will rejoice.... Let Christ alone reign and keep safe my royal halls! No evil spirit must enter the citadel of Romulus; my court must serve the Lord of Peace alone!" (Contra Orationem Symmachi, *2.737–38, 766–68). The triumph was short-lived, however. In 408, a concerted Visigothic siege of Rome was broken only through the payment of substantial ransom, and in 410, Alaric's forces entered the city, ransacking it for three days, an event that echoed loudly throughout the Mediterranean world.*

"Now I beseech you, brethren, ... that you all speak the same thing, and that there be no schisms among you, but that you be perfect in the same mind and in the same judgment."
1 Corinthians 1:10

Enlisting in the allegory here the composite beasts of pagan mythology—centaurs, minotaurs, and the like. In the allegory of Dante's Inferno *12, these beasts become guardians of the Circle of the Violent.*

Address from the tribunal. *Lyon, Bibliothèque de la Part-Dieu, P. A. 22, f. 11v (photo: IRHT-CNRS)*

With the Edict of Thessalonica, issued jointly by the emperors Gratian, Valentinian II, and Theodosius I on February 27, 380, the Trinitarian tenets of the Nicene Creed became the official orthodoxy of the Roman state: "Those who follow this rule [shall] espouse the name of Catholic Christians. But the others, who are raving madmen in our judgment, ... [shall] bear the infamy of their heretical teachings ... and suffer both the condemnation of God and the punishments that we ourselves inflict in accordance with Heaven's will." (Codex Theodosianus 16.1.2).

"No, love must fuse our understandings
And attune our lives to but a single aim,
For in division there is weakness.
And even as JESUS mediates God and man,
Conjoining with the Father what is mortal
And uniting deathless Spirit with the flesh
That a single God be both,
So a single spirit must accommodate
The action of our mind and body both
Within a single, self-consistent frame.

IN PRAISE OF PEACE

"The fullness of a Virtue's work is PEACE.
PEACE is the perfection of our labors,
The prize of the war we waged
And the dangers we faced.
In PEACE stars live and move across the sky,
In PEACE the things of earth stand fixed in place.
Without PEACE nothing is pleasing to God:
Your offering at his altar he will spurn
If your heart is clouded with anger
Against your brother.
Even should you deliver yourself
To the fires of martyrdom,

"If thou offer thy gift at the altar and remember that thy brother hath any thing against thee, leave thy offering ... and go first to be reconciled to thy brother...."
Matthew 5:23–24

"And if I should deliver my body to be burned, and have not charity, it profiteth me nothing. Charity is patient, is kind: charity envieth not, dealeth not perversely, is not puffed up, is not ambitious, seeketh not her own, is not easily provoked, thinketh no evil, rejoiceth not in iniquity but rejoiceth in the truth, beareth all things, believeth all things, hopeth all things, endureth all things."
1 Corinthians 13:3–7

It will profit you nothing to have spent
Your life for JESUS' sake
If you hold some remnant of uncharitable desire
Unquiet in your breast.
For PEACE is the end and sum of merit:
She does not swell with pride, she feels no envy,
She endures all things with patience,
Believes all things with faith,
Bears wrong with no resentment,
Forgives all offense, and pardons before
The sun can set on a lasting anger.
The proper worship of God begins with PEACE;
No sacrifice is sweeter to CHRIST,
No offering more acceptable at his altar.

"Let not the sun go down upon your anger."
Ephesians 4:26

"Now this you must understand:

"Even to snow-white doves God gives the power
To peer beneath the surface and discern
The false-feathered serpent in the nest.
But the wolf still devours the lambs of the fold
Under the fleecy cover of a sheep.

"Beware of false prophets, who come to you in the clothing of sheep, but inwardly they are ravening wolves."
Matthew 7:15

The play with near anagrams here (COLUBRUM, "serpent," *and* COLUMBA, "dove") *provides a brief textual model of the need for careful discrimination.*

THE STEALTH AND LIVING THREAT OF HERESY

"By just such subterfuge
Do ARIUS and PHOTINUS cloak themselves,
Two wolves of guile and menace;
And to the power of the stealthy hand
My recent danger and this flow of blood—
Though the wound itself is superficial—
Both can testify."

Two theologians whose doctrines especially regarding the status of the Son were condemned by the Catholic Church. Arius (d. 336) taught the subordination of the Son to the Father, and though surviving accounts of his teachings are sketchy and contradictory, it is likely that Photinus (d. 376) held that the Son was adopted, not begotten, by the Father. Despite its condemnation at the Council of Nicaea in 325 and again at the First Council of Constantinople in 381, Arianism in particular had a long and vigorous life, remaining the dominant form of Christianity among some Germanic peoples of western Europe as late as the seventh century.

And the people groan in sorrow.

THE INSTRUCTIONS OF TRUE FAITH

But TRUE FAITH tells them:
"No, you must not grieve:
This is a happy time. CONCORD was injured, true,
But FAITH has been preserved—or let me say
That CONCORD too is safe, my sister here beside me,
Laughing at her wounds, my dearest comfort
And salvation. There is nothing now to dread.

SOLOMON, FIRST BUILDER OF THE TEMPLE

"But there is a task, a great one, to perform
That has been left for this day of peace.
Wise SOLOMON first took it up,
Peaceful heir to a warrior's throne,
For DAVID's hands were stained with slaughter

1 Chronicles 28:2–3

And reeked of the blood of kings.
But when the blood of war is purged, *1 Kings 5:2–5*
Then may a temple be built, an altar founded
In a house of CHRIST covered in gold. *1 Kings 6:22*
So Jerusalem the glorious, the divine,
Received God in the temple, there to rest,
And the nomad Ark was settled near the altar.

Before its installation in the Holy of Holies of Solomon's temple, the Ark of the Covenant had been mounted on a cart and moved from place to place. It contained "the two tables of stone, which Moses put there at Horeb" (1 Kings 8:9). According to Hebrews 9:4, it also contained the staff of Aaron, which is put forward below as a prefiguration of the scepter of Wisdom.

"In our camp too let a blessed temple rise
And let the Almighty visit his Holy of Holies.
For why then have we fought, why driven back
The earthborn hosts of Sin
If the Son of Man cannot descend from heaven,
Enter the City of the Purified Body,
And find it properly adorned
With a glorious temple of light?
Before this we have labored hard in war,
One battle and another and another;
Now let the white robe of PEACE take up the task,
And let our armies at peace erect our temple."

THE NEW TEMPLE RISES

True Faith and Concord lay out the new building. *Paris, BnF Ms. lat. 15158, f. 62r*

The New Temple Rises

THE QUEEN DESCENDS AND CONCORD WITH HER,
Her sister and partner in the work.
Together they take a golden reed
And lay out the new temple on level ground:

Foursquare and regular,
Each face alike, each angle perfect,
Nothing to mar its symmetry.

THE TEMPLE GATES

Three gates in the east,
Three gates in the west,
Three gates in the north,
Three gates in the south,

And at the gates no building stones are laid,
But a single, huge, and glittering gem,
Hewn through with force and care,
Spans each doorway with a shining arch
And forms the entry court, one gem alone.

"The holy city … had a wall great and high, and had twelve gates, and at the gates twelve angels, and names written thereon, which are the names of the twelve tribes of Israel. On the east three gates, and on the north three gates, and on the south three gates, and on the west three gates. And the wall of the city had twelve foundations, and in them, the twelve names of the twelve apostles of the Lamb. And he that spoke with me had a golden reed to measure the city.… And the city lieth foursquare, and its length was as great as its breadth, and he measured the city with the reed for twelve thousand furlongs, and the length and breadth and height of it are equal. And he measured its wall at a hundred forty-four cubits.… And the building of the wall was of jasper,

(*continued on p. 132*)

And above the gates, inscribed in gold,
The twelve names of the apostolic senate;
For with these names the Spirit surrounds
The hidden places of the Soul
And through them summons chosen thoughts
Into the inmost part.

So man approaches the altar at the heart
By a trinity of paths
From each of the four sides
That comprise his bodily nature:
The morning sun of childhood,
The sultry heat that blisters adolescence,
The rich, full light of men at their prime,
The chill north wind that calls to holy rites.
And the four triads of names
Join at a crossroads at the center
To honor the twelve disciples of the King.

THE PHASES OF LIFE FIGURED BY THE ORIENTATION OF THE TEMPLE

And twelve gemstones of enormous size
Set within the fabric of the walls
Pour the living souls of colors from their depths:

(continued from p. 131)
and the city itself pure gold, like to clear glass. And the foundations of the wall of the city were adorned with all manner of precious stones. The first foundation was jasper, the second sapphire, the third a chalcedony, the fourth an emerald, the fifth sardonyx, the sixth sard, the seventh chrysolite, the eighth beryl, the ninth a topaz, the tenth a chrysoprase, the eleventh a jacinth, the twelfth an amethyst. And the twelve gates were twelve pearls, and every gate was of one pearl. And the street of the city was pure gold, as it were transparent glass."
Revelation 21:10–21

Concord and True Faith guiding the work. *St. Gallen, Stiftsbibliothek, Cod. Sang. 135, p. 435 (www.e-codices.ch/en/csg/0135/435)*

The temple rises. *Brussels, KBR Ms. 10066-77, f. 136v.*

THE GEMSTONES OF THE TEMPLE

SAPPHIRE next to CHRYSOLITE,
The goldstone, next to BERYL,
And the aura of the central stone
Continuously modulates the luster
Of the stones on either side;
CHALCEDONY next to JACINTH,
A deep blue pool, clear violet light;
AMETHYST by SARDONYX,
And JASPER, SARD, and TOPAZ
Broadcast their colors to adjacent stones;
And across them all, loose waves of EMERALD,
Spring grass growing bright on a prairie;
Then burning CHRYSOPRASE, green-gold,
A brilliant star among these brilliant stones.

"Pattern of Elysian hues! Once in Ordos my father, climbing a hill after a storm, inadvertently entered the base of a rainbow—the rarest occurrence!—and found himself in colored air, in a play of light as if in paradise. He took one more step—and left paradise."
Vladimir Nabokov, The Gift, *chap. 2*

And a great winch groans to lift them into place.

THE HOUSE OF WISDOM

Within this space is built a house
On seven pillars cut from purest crystal;
And a white stone is set over it,
Shaped into a cone above
But curved like a shell beneath,
A pearl of a thousand talents.

"Wisdom hath built herself a house, she hath hewn out her seven pillars."
Proverbs 9:1

"The kingdom of heaven is like unto a merchant seeking goodly pearls, who when he had found one pearl of great price, . . . sold all he had, and bought it."
Matthew 13:45–46

The temple of the Lord. *Brussels, KBR Ms. 9987-91, f. 127v*

The house of Wisdom. *Brussels, KBR Ms. 9987-91, f. 128v*

TRUE FAITH had bought this pearl,
Selling all she had, to place it here.
For here is the throne of WISDOM,
Here WISDOM directs the governance of her realm
And meditates new laws for humankind;
In her hands a scepter made by no art,
But a staff of living wood, cut from its stock,
Severed from earthly nourishment,
Yet burgeoning with perfect leaves
And bloodred roses twined with palest lilies,
And these blossoms do not wither on their stem.

". . . as white lilies redden bunched with roses."
Virgil, Aeneid *12.68–69*

Reversing the images both of King Latinus' staff in the mythical prehistory of Rome—"Never will it sprout leaves or branch. . . . Once a living tree, now an artist's hand has encased it in bronze for the elders of Latium to carry" (*Virgil,* Aeneid *12.207–11*)*—and, behind it, of Achilles' scepter at the pagan beginning of the epic tradition, "which will never again bear leaf nor branch since it was cut from its stock . . . , nor will it blossom now that bronze has stripped off leaf and bark. . . ."* (*Homer,* Iliad *1.234–37*)

The pattern for this scepter is AARON's staff,
Which put forth flowers, budding from dry bark,
Unfolding hope as it swelled into new fruit.

THE FIGURE OF AARON'S STAFF

The miracle of Aaron's flowering staff confirmed divine sanction for the priestly authority of the tribe of Levi (Numbers 17:1–10).

ENVOI

The poet offers thanks. *London, from the British Library Collection, Cotton MS Titus D XVI, f. 34r*

Envoi

Christ the Teacher

MOST GENEROUS OF TEACHERS, OUR CHRIST,
Most worthy to be honored, to be thanked,
Though our hearts are grimed with Sin—

You wanted us to learn about the dangers
Hidden in the envelope of flesh
And the doubtful chances of the struggling Soul.
We have learned that in the blindness of the heart
An ambivalent disposition is at war,
Laboring in successive conflicts;
And as the outcome varies, it will prosper,
Grow vigorous and upright,
Or else—when Virtues fail—it too will fail,
Be led away in bondage to the worse,
A slave to Sin, forsaking its salvation.

How often have we felt the Soul grow warm
With the flame of God when Sin is beaten back,
And then, that white joy past, how often felt

Our heavenly genius cool again and yield
To appetite.
Wars rage within our bones,
Cruel, desperate wars, and we do not see them.
Human nature is divided and it roils
In the violence that is born of this division.
For the flesh that is formed of clay
Presses down upon the soul,
But that spirit, born in the breath of God,
Still glows within the darkness
And it rejects the soiled body
Despite all that holds it.

"Cruel, desperate wars. . . ."
Virgil, Aeneid *6.86*

THE DIVIDED NATURE OF MAN

"And the Lord God formed man of the earth's clay and breathed into his nostrils the breath of life, and man became a living soul."
Genesis 2:7

So, light and shadow are at war within us,
And this doubleness gives rise to forces
That will not cease their strife until our God,
Our Christ, stands by us as Defender
To set the Virtues' gemstones into place
And, where Sin once held sway, to build his temple,
Crafting ornaments for the Soul from the display
Of our moral temper, ornaments
For Wisdom to delight in.
Rich Wisdom!
May she reign forever on her splendid throne.

Wisdom's eternal reign

"O the depth of the riches of the wisdom . . . of God!"
Romans 11:33

Translator's Afterword

Prudentius was one of the key transitional figures of European literature, thoroughly at home in the poetic world of Virgil and Horace but pointing in a unique way to the work of such figures as Dante, Jean de Meun, Chaucer, Spenser, and even Milton. His work includes hymns and other devotional poetry, as well as several verse treatises in defense of the Catholic doctrine established only in his adulthood as the official orthodoxy of the Roman state. His most far-reaching work, though, is the poem translated here as *SoulStrife*, which literally renders its original Greek title, *Psychomachia*. It is a brisk poem of just under a thousand lines, lively and ironic, sometimes gruesome in its violence, sometimes comic, sometimes grim, clearly invoking the epic tradition in much of its language and narrative motifs. But it is not so much as narrative that the poem has made its mark. During the early Middle Ages in particular, the *Psychomachia* developed an extraordinary popularity, its influence widely felt, partly for its easily communicated moral lessons, partly for its highly charged visual tableaux, and partly for the exemplary ways it reads and interprets other texts, both biblical and secular, and calls out to be read in its turn. As its translator, I took it as my first responsibility to address the contemporary experience of reading such a poem.

Prudentius wrote a dense poetic Latin, syntactically thorny, semantically layered, and highly rhetorical, something of a challenge to readers then and now. He was free with puns, anagrams, etymological play, and similar devices that exploit the properties of individual words. He introduced codes, both linguistic and numeric, and set puzzles for readers to solve. Notably, his text is crowded with associations and the living memory of earlier texts, an integral feature of the poem that makes further demands on the attention of a reader already engaged on all sides. Verse like this, however well it works in Latin, tends to congeal in translation and cloud over. One of my early concerns, then, was finding ways to maintain the fluidity of the poem and the clarity of its argument, a process that involved the resources of both language and visual design. I set out to smooth the twistier bits of the poem's Latin syntax—sometimes simply by segmenting a sentence or two and reordering the parts—and streamlined a few of the plumpest portions of its set-piece rhetoric just to keep things moving. For both the Latin trimeters of the foreword and the longer hexameter lines of the poem proper, I used meters I hoped were flexible enough to keep up an energetic, sometimes even fidgety, pace while remaining capable of the full-throated stateliness much of the poem requires. In diction, I generally followed Prudentius, aiming for a precise, relatively formal, and recognizably literary language, although I was more sparing than he was in the use of out-of-the-way vocabulary—neologisms, archaisms, rare or foreign words, and the like—cautious of its tendency to stop the show. To help clarify the overarching argument, I took the easy step of articulating the poem visually at its obvious main junctures, defining sections with their own headings, "Invocation," "First Combat," and so on, twelve in all, following the poet's own separate foreword. And within each section, I adopted the manuscript convention of marginal rubrics to orient a reader further.

The notes were to handle much of the rest. One of their chief functions was as a readily accessible bank of associations for the poem's present readers. There are a few instances where a note will point out a textual variant, offer historical or linguistic data, or respond at paragraph length to a local difficulty in the text, but in the main, the notes consider the poem's relationship to other texts. They identify literary sources and parallels, most often only briefly, but when the poem's involvement with the cited text is fuller or more complex, they will quote and occasionally quote at length. Some seek to give a sense of the traditions of allegory and of ethical discourse, both formal and informal, in which the poem has a significant place; since neither tradition began or ended with Prudentius, they freely cite both earlier and later exponents, Ambrose along with Dante, Seneca along with Spinoza, Tertullian along with William Burroughs and *The New York Times*. Others trace, in greater detail, the poem's connections with biblical texts or the centuries-old tradition of secular Roman literature, Virgil's poetry in particular, with which Prudentius had a special bone to pick. The notes try not to argue but rely on juxtaposition and direct quotation as much as possible.

I preferred marginal annotation to either foot- or endnotes because of what it implies for the process of reading. Most obvious, of course, is the ease of consultation it allows, mimicking the speed and operation of memory and setting up the possibility of direct, even stark, comparisons between the poetic text at hand and the passages cited for reference. This prompted me to focus in a practical way on a problem common to all literary translation but especially prominent in the case of Roman literature with its centuries of increasingly retrospective writing. Translation works with historical connections (or disjunctions) between languages all the time; that is just part of its job. But how does it, how can it represent in one language (here, English) historical connections—echoes, allusions, repetitions, recollections—that exist by their nature only *within* another (here, Latin)? My own response was to turn all the texts into English ones, translating the marginal texts in close tandem with the poem until their connections in English gave a reasonably good clue to the nature and extent of the connections in Latin—precise verbal or rhetorical replication, more general paraphrase, thematic coincidence, or any shade of resemblance in between. I am responsible, then, for the translation of all passages cited in the margins, although I closely modeled quotations of the Bible on the Douay-Rheims version (as revised by Richard Challoner, 1749–52), both for its dedication to the Latin text and the familiar feel of its rhetoric, instantly recognizable as "biblical."

Two other effects are perhaps more intimate. First, the format implicitly raises the status of the notes, asserting their importance by their placement—at times even emphatically, as on those pages where text and gloss jostle each other for space and attention—and bringing to prominence the primary act of reading, which any set of notes, however incomplete or idiosyncratic, is bound to represent. Annotation becomes more than the modest handmaid of the text, aspiring instead to a kind of partnership, if not precisely with the poem then at least with the poem's translation. For a latecomer text like the *Psychomachia*, with its long history of reception and a hefty stake in the problems and possibilities of reading, I think this is more than fitting. And second, the marginal apparatus here directly affects the pace and rhythm of reading the central text, inevitably slowing it down with manifold distractions and forestalling any prospect of smooth and measured progress. Readers scan the pages in countless unpredictable patterns, not simply left to right and top to bottom, but skipping from right across to left again, back up and across, and then again down—perceiving, remembering, connecting, testing, pausing, reconsidering—turning linear sequence into something more complex. With this, the ensemble of translation and notes may do what the translation alone will not, that is, call for a version of the careful, textured reading required by the Latin original and offer a reminder, if one is ever needed, how close a collaboration of eye and mind the process of reading is.

I often got the sense as I was working that the *Psychomachia* would rather be a painting than a poem. There is the ethical abstraction given expression in space with distinct shape, color, hairstyle, face—the first principle of its allegory. There is the narrative flattened into discrete panels reminiscent of the nave mosaics of early churches or the later brilliance of stained glass. There is the vivid pictorial description that seems to demand illustration of both the poem's great spurts of violence and the small, inconsequential details that nonetheless stick in a reader's mind: the newly freed Lot straightening his neck, the oil-slicked hair of Riotous Living, the gleam of her chariot, the tender feet of Pleasure pricked by thorns. There is the reassertion of sight as the master metaphor for understanding, its failure as the masquerade of Greed confounds the armies, its success as the Virtues suss out Heresy through a set of visual signs, and its somewhat disconcerting triumph as the scrutiny of Concord comes to probe every member of the camp, every hidden part of the soul. There is also the large and varied lexicon of visual appearance: "the faces of the Virtues," "the living souls of colors," "the display of moral temper," "figure," "form." There is the repeated injunction laid on the reader to *see*. There are things that sight can do and words cannot.

The illustrations included in this book (which document a further mode of reading the poem) were selected from manuscripts of the *Psychomachia* dating from the late ninth to the thirteenth century. For their permission to reproduce images of texts in their keeping, I gratefully acknowledge the following institutions and their staffs: the British Library in London (with special thanks to licensing assistant Katerina Borisova, who eased every step), the Bibliothèque de la Part-Dieu in Lyon, the Koninklijke Bibliotheek van Belgie (KBR) in Brussels, the Stiftsbibliothek in St. Gallen, and the Bibliothèque nationale de France in Paris. For making reproductions of the Lyon manuscript freely available, I thank the Institut de Recherche et d'Histoire des Textes of the Centre national de la Recherche scientifique.

I am also grateful to individuals closer to home whose help, encouragement, and criticism have gone into making this book what it is. I thank Sara Ahbel-Rappe for her brilliant and groundbreaking introduction; Sarah Klitenic Wear of Franciscan University for her imaginative support of the project, her sympathetic insight, and her extraordinary patience over a long period; and Rebecca Schreiber for the handsome design of this volume. I thank Adam Thorburn and Jorie Woods for their early critical readings of the translation, and I am grateful to David Thorburn for his penetrating reading of both the text and its auxiliary material. Thanks also to Lloyd Gerson, Stanley Lombardo, and Bruce O'Brien for opening doors I could not have opened on my own. As ever, my deepest gratitude goes to Debra Nails.

The book is inscribed to Martha Malamud, the finest reader of Prudentius around and a generous, good friend of many years.

Lot in his freedom. *Lyon, Bibliothèque de la Part-Dieu, P. A. 22, f. 3v (photo: IRHT-CNRS)*